I have watched Dr. Sweeting, studied him, worked for him, listened to him, and read his works. The wisdom from this book is from the heart of God. He lives what he writes. Joy exudes from his life. Read this book and follow his counsel. Joy will be evident in your life.

Dr. Thomas S. Fortson
Executive Vice President
Promise Keepers

Since childhood, I have aspired to one day be a "godly old lady"! So I was delighted to learn that Dr. Sweeting—a true role model—had come up with a road map for my journey. As the title suggest, Dr. Sweeting is convinced that aging is a process that can be anticipated rather than dreaded— that the blessings of the sunset season of life can outweigh the burdens. In his warm, winsome way that includes a wonderful blend of humor and illustrations, he shares practical insights that have been birthed out of his many years of fruitful life and ministry. This book will be an encouragement and help to every believer, regardless of age, who wants to "finish well" for the glory of God.

Nancy Leigh DeMoss
Author and teacher for
Revive Our Hearts radio program

Dr. George Sweeting has been my mentor and a man I have greatly admired down through the years. He is a living example of growing old and retiring with joy. And much of it comes from a very fruitful and productive life with the Lord. The Bible speaks in Psalm 92:14 of aging, "They shall still

bring forth fruit in old age; they shall be fat and flourishing"
and again in Isaiah 46:4, "And even to your old age I am
he; and even to hoar hairs will I carry you; I have made, and
I will bear, even I will carry you. I will deliver you."

Rev. Clay Evans
Founder & Senior Pastor,
Fellowship Missionary Baptist Church
Chicago, IL

THE JOYS OF SUCCESSFUL AGING

Finishing with Grace

George Sweeting

NORTHFIELD PUBLISHING
CHICAGO

All Scripture quotations unless otherwise indicated are taken from the *New King James Version*. Copyright © 1982 by Thomas Nelson, Inc. Used by permission. All rights reserved.

Scripture quotations marked NIV are taken from the *Holy Bible, New International Version*®. NIV®. Copyright © 1973, 1978, 1984 by International Bible Society. Used by permission of Zondervan Publishing House. All rights reserved.

The "NIV" and "New International Version" trademarks are registered in the United States Patent and Trademark Office by International Bible Society. Use of either trademark requires permission of International Bible Society.

Scripture quotations marked NASB are taken from the *New American Standard Bible*®. © Copyright The Lockman Foundation 1960, 1962, 1963, 1968, 1971, 1972, 1973, 1977, 1995. Used by permission.

Scripture quotations marked KJV are taken from the King James Version.

Editorial services by:
Julie-Allyson Ieron, Joy Media

Grateful acknowledgment is hereby expressed to those who have granted permission to include copyrighted materials in this book. Any inadvertent omission will be gladly corrected in future editions.

Library of Congress Cataloging-in-Publication Data

Sweeting, George, 1924–
    The joys of successful aging : finishing with grace / George Sweeting.
       p. cm.
    Includes bibliographical references.
    ISBN 1-881273-13-X
    1. Christian aged--Religious life. 2. Aging--Religious aspects--Christianity. I. Title.

BV4580 .S94 2002
248.8′5--dc21

                                                                    2002070967

1 3 5 7 9 10 8 6 4 2

Printed in the United States of America

This book is affectionately dedicated to our grandchildren:

Christopher
Erika
Aubrey
James
Katelyn
Nathan
Jonathan
Joshua
Jeremiah
Julianna

Special appreciation is offered

To Sonja Goppert for her superb help in preparing this manuscript.

To my son Dr. Donald Sweeting for reviewing the manuscript and suggesting ways to improve it.

To Dr. Brett Abernathy for reviewing chapters 3, 4, 5, and 6 from his perspectve as a medical doctor, a warm thank you.

CONTENTS

꩜

PREFACE

J oy and aging are seldom linked together; however I
have discovered many unexpected joys in my senior
years.

Through no credit of my own, I was born with a
happy disposition. As a child, I must confess I lived on
the sunny side of the street. I was also a giggler and was
occasionally asked to leave the classroom until I could
compose myself. Try as I would, when I would reenter
the room, the class would erupt in laughter . . . causing
me to return to the hallway.

Authentic joy, of course, has nothing to do with
brightness of disposition or personality. Authentic joy
comes from a spiritual relationship; so that joy is possible
even amid earthly limitations. You *can* age with joy and
finish with grace. The word *grace* comes from the Greek

word *charis* suggesting unmerited favor. There are no prerequisites to grace. As Augustine said, "It will not be the grace of God in any way, unless it has been gratuitous in every way."

Caleb, of Old Testament fame, is one of the theme characters of this book. At age eighty-five, when many people dream of retirement, Caleb was going strong. In fact he claimed to be as strong to serve at age eighty-five as he was at age forty (Josh. 14:11).

Rather than seeking security and ease, he asked for an enemy-infested mountain, so he could give it as an inheritance to his children and grandchildren. Caleb is an authentic role model for all who want to age successfully. His last years were his best . . . and they can be your best, as well!

We don't stop laughing because we grow old;
we grow old because we stop laughing.

ANONYMOUS

❧

A chuckle a day may not keep the doctor away,
but it sure does make those times in life's waiting room
a little more bearable.

ANNE WILSON SCHAEF

❧

Laughter is like changing a baby's diaper—
it doesn't permanently solve a thing, but it does
make life more acceptable for a while.

ANONYMOUS

❧

If I were given an opportunity to present a gift to
the next generation, it would be the ability
for each individual to learn to laugh at himself.

CHARLES SCHULZ

*Gentlemen, why don't you laugh? With the
fearful strain that is upon me night and day,
if I did not laugh, I should die.
You need this medicine as much as I do.*

ABRAHAM LINCOLN

*There is a time for everything, . . . a time to weep and a time
to laugh.*

ECCLESIASTES 3:1, 4 (NIV)

1

❧

LIGHTEN UP

Though the subject of aging is seldom presented with excitement, let alone humor, I have chosen for the sake of encouragement to begin on the lighter side. Humor combats stress and helps us to creatively cope with life. The last years of life can be joyful and fulfilling; though for some, aging is a challenge.

A visitor at a church social asked the pastor to guess her age. When he hesitated, she said, "Oh, you must have some idea."

"I have two ideas," he admitted. "My problem is: I can't decide whether to make you ten years younger because of your looks, or ten years older because of your charm."

An aging wife inquired of her husband, "Will you love me when I'm old, gray, and wrinkled?"

To which he answered, "I do."

HOW TO TELL YOU'RE GETTING OLDER

The newspaper carried an article by that title. Here are some of the answers:

1. When your knees buckle . . . and your belt won't.
2. When you get into a rocking chair . . . and can't get it rocking.
3. When everything hurts and what doesn't hurt . . . doesn't work.
4. When you bend over to tie your shoelaces and you think . . . *Is there anything else I ought to do while I'm down here?*
5. When the little old lady you help cross the street . . . is your wife.
6. When year by year your feet seem farther from your hands.
7. When a handsome man or a pretty girl passes . . . and you don't even notice.
8. When, if you're a man, more hair grows out of your ears than on your head.
9. When you stand on one leg . . . and can't get your pants on.
10. When it costs more for your birthday candles . . . than for the cake.
11. When you have so many liver spots on your hand . . . that it looks like speckled sausage.
12. And when you pray for a good prune juice harvest . . . whatever that means.[1]

I was born on October 1, 1924, the same day and year as former President Jimmy Carter. I share the year of my birth so you will know that I too am a senior and have experienced some of the ups and downs of life. Besides being a senior, twice I have survived cancer.

At age twenty, I was told I had testicular cancer and probably wouldn't see the year out. I was also told that if I lived, it would be unlikely that I would ever father children. The year was 1944. My doctor was Titus Johnson of Chicago's Swedish Covenant Hospital. Following two surgeries and thirty radiation treatments, I slowly regained my health. During the first two years, I received a thorough physical examination every six months and since then, a yearly checkup. My annual check up has turned out to be a blessing in disguise, enabling me to catch physical problems in their early stages. And despite Dr. Johnson's predictions, my wife and I were blessed with four sons.

As a teenager, I was naïve concerning my health. Sickness taught me to listen to my body. This has been a lifesaver for me. They say if you want to live long, you need to be sick early. Though I'm not sure that's true, my cancer made me aware of my human frailty and also some essentials of good health. I'm sincerely thankful for the life-threatening experience of testicular cancer because of the lessons I learned.

Once again, at age fifty-nine, after a routine transurethral resection of the prostate, cancer cells were discovered. Again, I chose to have thirty radiation treatments. That was nearly twenty years ago, and my present PSA is an amazing .01.

I share this with you first of all because I have learned that cancer . . . does not necessarily mean death. Second, even though I have faced the ravages of disease and pain, through it all I have known a measure of usefulness and much joy. So think of me as an old friend who, having weathered some of the storms of life ... wants to share a little advice.

USE IT ... OR LOSE IT

Continual involvement with life is a major requirement for successful aging. Getting older is like waterskiing: When you slow down, you go down. So ... keep on going!

The theme of this book is illustrated in the life of Caleb (Numbers 13–14; Joshua 14). Early in life, he cast his lot with the famous tribe of Judah and was chosen to represent them. He also identified with the minority when ten of the twelve spies brought back a negative report of the Promised Land. Caleb courageously urged the people to "go up at once and take possession" (Numbers 13:30). He told the people not to fear but to move forward. He was *fully involved* at age forty (Joshua 14:7) and fully involved at age eighty-five (v. 10). In fact, at age eighty-five he displayed the optimism of a twenty-year-old. He professed to be "as strong this day as on the day that Moses sent me" (verse 11). He was *involved* with life in his youth, during the middle years, and in old age. His *involvement* and *optimism* are two essentials for longevity.

When the children of Israel conquered the land, Caleb, at age eighty-five, made a megarequest concerning the future: "Now ... *give me this mountain.* ... It may be that the Lord will be with me, and I shall be able to drive them out as the Lord said" (Joshua 14:12, italics added). At age eighty-five, Caleb overcame the inhabitants and received Hebron as an inheritance for his children, grandchildren and great-grandchildren. His last years were his best. Caleb was involved in a cause bigger than himself. Caleb finished with grace.

Dr. Michael DeBakey offers a spectacular example of successful aging. This pioneering heart surgeon has been a leader in his field for more than fifty years. At age eighty-nine, he supervised open-heart surgery on Boris Yeltsin, then president of Russia. His next goal was to perfect a new artificial heart.

At an age when many of his contemporaries would have given up, he walked briskly, stood erect, and offered a firm handshake. His lifestyle is simple. He rises at 5 A.M., eats a light breakfast of fruit, skims the newspaper, and goes off to work consulting, reading, operating, and writing.

He feels the most important steps to extending life are:

1. **Control hypertension,** which can be done in most cases through medication.
2. **Refrain from smoking,** which is responsible for 20 percent of all deaths from heart disease and 50 percent of all cancer deaths.
3. **Eat a diet low in fat** to reduce the chances of arteriosclerosis and heart disease. (My doctor is fond of reminding me: "Fat rats in experiments die before skinny rats.")

When Dr. DeBakey was asked how he keeps active he answered, "We say of muscles, 'Use it or lose it.' The same thing applies to the mind; the more you use it, the better it functions. It is better to be mentally active than to be a couch potato."[2]

Dr. DeBakey doesn't see his passion as the mere extending of life. "The important thing isn't the actual number of years but to function well, both mentally and physically. That's what constitutes life. These people who linger for years, unable to enjoy life—I call that the prolongation of death."[3]

In an interview for *Esquire* magazine, DeBakey displayed

the excitement and vision of a young man. When asked about the future he answered, "This new century that we're in is going to be one of the most exciting in all history. The medical advances that have taken place since World War II are amazing. I would say this is the best time in the history of the world to be a six-year-old, oh yes. By far, by far."[4]

PEACE AMID LOSS

My Scottish mother experienced a lifetime of negatives. Her mother, Annie McKerrow Irving, died giving birth to her third child, leaving her husband, George Irving, to care for my mother, her brother, Isaac, and the newborn, Annie.

Life was hard in their Carstairs Junction home in Scotland. Her father found it impossible to work and handle his three young children as a single parent. At first, he hired a live-in housekeeper who, along with her children, moved in. Eventually, George Irving married a widow with three children and brought them into the household. However, living conditions were so stressful that my mother's brother, Isaac, at fourteen, left home and joined the British navy, while her sister, Annie, ran away, never to be heard from again.

Though my mother's childhood had great sorrow, she experienced a marvelous change in her teens. An acquaintance, Jesse Kay, whom I met decades later, began a girl's club in Carstairs Junction. After several visits to the club, my mother, Mary Rodger Irving, experienced a spiritual awakening. As a teenager, she became bright, winsome, and committed to growth. Her faith made her home situation tolerable.

My father, William Sweeting, after returning from fighting for three years in Belgium in World War I with the Royal

British Engineers, picked up his trade as a stonemason. His work brought him to Carstairs Junction, where he helped build a large stone bridge over the town's railroad station. There my parents met. My mother quickly shared her faith, telling of her life's transformation. She also urged my father to visit two centers in Glasgow, called Bethany Hall and Tent Hall, where he could hear more about the new life she had discovered.

Because of my father's war experiences and the chaos of life in general, he was eager to visit Bethany Hall, where he also experienced a spiritual transformation. The change in his life was so dramatic that his father feared he would become a fanatic. His conversion led to eventual courtship with my mother and to marriage to Mary Rodger Irving of Carstairs Junction in 1920.

Tired of Europe's wars and eager to better themselves, they immigrated to the United States in 1923.

Though my father was the unquestioned head of the home, my mother was "the heart of our home." Along with a sincere faith, she possessed a loving, cheerful disposition. She gave birth to six children: William, Anne, George, Norman, Mary, and Martha.

In the 1940s, she was afflicted with rheumatoid arthritis. At times, her condition was so severe that she was bedfast for months and even years. Her hands were deformed and her joints gnarled, yet even in suffering she was attractive. With the advent of cortisone, she managed with great difficulty to get about the home.

Her faith was obvious to all who came to visit. Amid constant pain and meager assets, she displayed a joyful spirit and a gentle sense of humor during forty years of suffering. Her winsomeness in sickness was not due to her personality but the result of trust. She believed that because God allowed adversity He would give equal grace. I saw firsthand that it is possible . . . amid suffering . . . to age with joy and finish with grace.

Comedian Woody Allen once quipped, "Eighty percent of success is in . . . showing up." Showing up is important, but CONTINUED INVOLVEMENT with life, even in pain and loss, is all-important to successful aging.

So keep on keeping on. Use it . . . or lose it! Keep involved even in your trials, and don't take yourself too seriously.

Lighten up!

Anybody who can still do at sixty . . .
what he was doing at twenty . . .
wasn't doing much at twenty.

FORMER PRESIDENT JIMMY CARTER,
The Virtues of Aging, 48

I don't feel like an old man. I feel like a young man . . .
who has something the matter with him.

BRUCE BLIVEN

The positive benefits of religion in the lives of elderly
adults are many. Researchers at Georgetown University
reviewed over 200 studies of religion and health. They
found that three-fourths of the studies revealed the positive
effects of religion on drug abuse, depression,
blood pressure, and heart disease. Other researchers have
found that the greater the religious involvement
of elderly people, the greater their self-esteem.

DONALD H. KAUSLER AND BARRY C. KAUSLER[1]

2

PEOPLE OF FAITH
TEND TO LIVE LONGER

While I was appearing on a talk show with educators and clergy, the host read a quotation from *USA Today* claiming that people of religious faith tend to live longer than people of no faith. The host, though skeptical, asked if there was any validity to such a statement. Because I had read the same article and felt the statement was valid, I volunteered to respond. The moderator pointed at me and said, "Elucidate." I proceeded to give five reasons why I agreed.

1. People of faith view the physical body as God's temple.

People of the Judeo-Christian faith believe all men and women are created in the image of God (Genesis 1:27). They also embrace the words of the psalmist,

"You have made him a little lower than the angels, and You have crowned him with glory and honor" (Psalm 8:5). The New Testament also teaches that the human body is "the temple of God" (1 Corinthians 3:16–17) and should not be defiled. In fact, neglect of the body insures a divine penalty (verse 17).

Comedian Bill Cosby occasionally refers to physical fitness as "temple keeping," and I understand why. Our bodies are special gifts that are viewed as sacred.

Other religious faiths also hold a high view of the body and, for the most part, consider the body as a divine gift. If people believe God dwells in them, it makes a megadifference in how they treat their bodies.

Decades before the Surgeon General warned of the dangers of tobacco, millions of people of faith abstained from smoking because they felt tobacco was harmful to the body. This application was also made to drugs in general. It extended to moderation in eating, sleeping, and life as a whole. Granted, some carried these prohibitions to extremes; however, in general they were reasonably applied.

According to a Gallup Poll, 85 percent of those who responded believe physical health depends largely on how people care for their bodies. In other words, the individual makes a contribution to good health. We choose to treat the body with care and respect, *especially* if we believe the body is *sacred*. For this reason alone, people of faith tend to live longer.

2. People of faith ultimately trust God.

This mindset is expressed in phrases like, "God willing" or "if God wills." People of faith are encouraged to commit everything in life to a caring, all-wise, all-powerful God. In other

words, sufficient grace will be given for whatever He allows. National polls affirm that 80 percent of people over age sixty-five claim that religious beliefs are important in their lives.

Life, though enjoyable, isn't easy. In fact, life is difficult. However, people of faith don't live life alone. They find strength in words like, "O Lord, You have searched me and known me . . . and are acquainted with all my ways" (Psalm 139:1, 3). Or, "all things work together for good to those who love God, to those who are the called according to His purpose" (Romans 8:28). Promises like these enable people to transcend the limitations and losses of life.

Joseph, of the Old Testament, illustrates this attitude. As a boy he dreamed of future greatness, even though his dreams did not include the hardships he would endure before he would experience greatness. Joseph's brothers hated him because of his dreams of superiority and eventually sold him to some Midianites (Genesis 37:27–28). In Egypt, he gradually achieved success in the house of Potiphar, only to be abused by his employer's wife. This was followed by banishment to a dungeon for thirteen years.

Despite huge obstacles, Joseph believed God was in charge and that even his troubles were part of a divine preparation for future success and leadership. Ultimately, Joseph was reunited with his brothers. In the meantime, Joseph had risen to become leader of Egypt, second only to Pharoah. When Joseph met his brothers, they fell before him in terror. Then Joseph said to them, "You meant evil against me; but God meant it for good, in order to bring it about as it is this day, to save many people alive" (Genesis 50:20). Joseph's faith sustained him for a lifetime and enabled him to survive.

Likewise, on November 21, 2001, *USA Today* recalled Lisa

Beamer's faith in the light of the crash of Flight 93, September 11, 2001.

> Terrorists took Lisa Beamer's husband from her, but she refuses to forfeit her zest for life or faith in God.
>
> She lost her husband Todd, after he and others on Flight 93 battled hijackers for control of their plane. Although it crashed, killing all 44 aboard, the aircraft never hit its Washington, D.C., target.
>
> Now Beamer, mother of two small boys and expecting again in January, is determined to see that terrorists also miss the mark to wreck her life and the future of the children whose parents perished on the plane.
>
> Speaking of her husband's death, Lisa said, *"God ultimately has a plan. He takes us where we need to be."*[2]

People of faith, though not exempt from tragedy, ultimately commit their struggles to a sovereign God who is in charge of all of life. Often I have quoted, "It is vain for you to rise up early, to sit up late, to eat the bread of sorrows; for . . . He gives His beloved sleep" (Psalm 127:2).

Dr. Snowdon, in his book *Aging with Grace*, describes his careful study of an order of nuns and applies his findings to what we can learn about health and longevity. Though he freely admits this can't be scientifically tested, after years of observation he attributes their vigor, good health, and longevity to their faith, which serves as a shield against the inevitable tragedies of life.[3] Snowdon also believes there is growing evidence of the value of prayer, meditation, and faith as it relates to aging.

Herbert Benson of Harvard Medical School has written that frequent prayer can reduce pain in cancer patients and even lower blood pressure.[4]

3. People of faith are part of a large extended family.

Loneliness is the first thing God called "not good" in the book of Genesis, and yet it is part of human experience. Loneliness is defined as a feeling of separation, isolation, and distress.

A Harris survey revealed that the proportion of elderly people experiencing loneliness is substantial. In fact, loneliness is ranked high among the most serious problems older people believe to confront them . . . The probable causes of loneliness for elderly people were investigated by researchers at the University of South Carolina. Information was obtained from nearly 3,000 individuals aged 65 and older. A number of conditions were found to contribute to the loneliness experienced by many elderly people. However, the most important contributor was a low level of social fulfillment. Reduced social fulfillment means that they do not have enough to do to keep busy, and they do not feel needed. Among the other conditions contributing to loneliness of elderly people are changed marital status, reduced income, anxiety, frequency of telephone contact, and poor health. However, the effects of these other contributors are largely indirect: that is, they affect loneliness largely by way of their negative influences on social fulfillment.[5]

DONALD H. KAUSLER AND BARRY C. KAUSLER

Loneliness exists in part because life is a journey. In his well-known classic work *The Confessions of St. Augustine,*

Augustine wrote, "You have made us for Yourself, and our hearts are restless until they find peace in You."

An older friend said, "I'm not afraid of dying, but I am afraid of living 'til I die."

The brilliant Albert Einstein, speaking of loneliness, said, "It's strange to be known universally, and yet be so lonely." Though people of faith experience loneliness as well, it is possible for them to enjoy the support and relationship of a world-wide spiritual family of like-minded people. This oneness is further experienced in local church gatherings where real people are much like family. People need people, and the lack of relationship kills. Centenarians are almost never "loners." Loneliness appears to attract illness and in some cases even promotes early death.

David Snowdon, in *Aging with Grace,* speaks forcibly about the strength of community in the Nuns' study.[6]

In general, people connected with others through marriage, friendships, clubs, teams, and especially houses of worship, live longer. People of faith are not only part of a mega human family, but they are also related to a universal spiritual family.

We never outgrow our need for others. In fact, giving ourselves to help others is even more life building than receiving help from others. The law of living is giving.

4. People of faith continue their involvement with life in their places of worship.

In a seven-year study of seniors by the Center for Health Sciences/Institute for the Study of Human Knowledge, religious involvement was linked to less physical disability and less depression. A variety of studies suggest that religious belief and practice is also associated with less risk of self-destructive behaviors (smoking, drug and alcohol abuse, suicide), less perceived stress, and greater overall life satisfaction.

Involvement with all ages in a local place of service is life building and life extending. Places of worship have more individuals serving in their senior years than any other organizations. Claude Pepper, onetime representative for the state of Florida and onetime chairman of the House Select Committee on Aging, commented that, "Life is like riding a bicycle. You don't fall off unless you stop pedaling."

So keep pedaling. Keep involved. Activity is crucial. Seniors need to be pushed to stay involved. Involvement with all ages of people is a major factor in successful aging.

5. *People of faith tend to live longer* specifically *because of* their faith.

Caleb, our theme person, exemplifies three longevity traits but none more than his dynamic faith. (Chapter 8 will explore this in greater detail.)

In *The Graying of America,* the authors ask,

> Does religion actually serve to improve the health of elderly people? Over 10 years of studies at various university hospitals has indicated that, regardless of the nature of a person's religious preference, people who have a deep religious faith seem to get sick less often and get better faster when they do get sick than people with much less religious faith. Those with a strong religious faith have also been found to have lower rates of heart disease, stroke, and cancer. . . . The higher survival rate for frequent church attenders was especially characteristic of women,

but it did apply to men as well. Most important, the difference in survival rates held up even after controlling for differences between frequent and less frequent attenders in health and health practices. Not surprisingly, about 30 of the 125 accredited medical schools in the United States have included religious or spiritual teaching in their curricula.[7]

Others also affirm the results of faith on good health and healing. Dr. Herbert Benson, of Harvard Medical School, speaks of the Faith Factor. He highlights this in his book, *Beyond the Relaxation Response,* as a means of natural healing that results from:

1. A strong personal belief system that accepts the importance of caring for the body, and
2. The practice of prayer and meditation as part of those beliefs.[8]

Overwhelming evidence points to a strong relationship between faith and good health.[9]

I have used the phrase "people of faith" as it applies to all people who hold deep religious beliefs. However, as a Christian minister and educator for five decades, faith for me has its roots in the Bible, the inspired Word of God.

At this point, because I had taken a good portion of the time, the moderator lifted his hands in a gesture of surrender, saying, "You've made a believer out of me."

The following chapters will explore these themes in detail. I sincerely believe that your last years can be your best.

JOHN ANDERSON MY JO

John Anderson my jo, John,
When we were first acquent;
Your locks were like the raven,
Your bony brow was brent;

But now your brow is beld, John,
Your locks are like the snaw;
But blessings on your frosty pow,
John Anderson my Jo.

John Anderson my jo, John,
We clamb the hill the gither;
And monie a canty day, John,
We've had wi' ane anither;

Now we maun totter down, John,
And hand in hand we'll go;
And sleep the gither at the foot,
John Anderson my Jo.

ROBERT BURNS[10]

*The good news is that moderate, regular exercise has many
of the benefits of more strenuous athletics. The bad news,
all too familiar, is that most older men and women do not
engage even in moderate exercise on a regular basis.*

JOHN W. ROWE AND ROBERT L. KAHN[1]

*The cure for age . . . is interest, enthusiasm, and work.
Life's evening will take its character from the day
which has preceded it. You will always find joy
in the evening . . . if you've spent the day well.*

GEORGE MATHESON

*Do you not know that your body is the temple
of the Holy Spirit who is in you, whom you have
from God, and you are not your own?
For you were bought at a price; therefore glorify God
in your body and in your spirit, which are God's.*

1 CORINTHIANS 6:19–20

3

TEMPLE KEEPING

Comedian Bill Cosby, in his best-selling book *Time Flies,* enthusiastically shares some of his aging stories. He begins, "Temple was not just my college but a description of my body as well." Being a native of Philadelphia and a former student at Temple University, he tells how his onetime muscular, sleek body began to resemble his father's size and shape. Wistfully he asks, "What had happened to the temple?" He concludes that his body was being vandalized by time and attacked by an enemy called aging. I smiled as Cosby described the ritual of taking his shoes off and praying for "longer arms" so that he wouldn't feel like he was just about to give birth. With great humor he watches his body change from "a temple," to what he calls, "a storefront church."[2]

People of faith believe that men and women are made in the image of God (Genesis 1:26–27). Many go a step further and claim that the body is specifically "the temple of God," and God's Spirit indwells them. If this is so, then there are enormous implications concerning how the body is treated. The apostle Paul reminds the people of the city of Corinth, "You were bought at a price. Therefore *honor God with your body*" (1 Corinthians 6:20 NIV, italics added).

Temple keeping includes a broad area of stewardship. However, I want to highlight three areas: eating, exercise, and emotions.

YOU ARE WHAT YOU EAT

That was the title of a book I read in the 1960s. Though I have forgotten much of its information, I began to look at what I ate as essential to good health. Recent years have affirmed the fact that our eating habits are either life building or life destroying. After receiving a sizeable amount of scientific evidence, the American Heart Association concludes that *eating right is essential to good health*. It claims what we eat plays a major role in whether or not we will develop certain types of cancer.[3]

There are many choice books by experts on the subject of eating. Many of them offer similar kinds of advice. For example, authorities advocate that we:

1. Drink plenty of water each day. At least a quart but preferably two quarts of water per day. It's the best drink around. It gives a feeling of fullness with no calories. "Older people, on the average, need six to eight cups of water per day to maintain normal body functions."[4]

2. Eat foods low in fat and cholesterol.
3. Eat more high-fiber foods, as experts tell us they appear to lower cholesterol.
4. Eat lots of fruits and vegetables.
5. Limit your consumption of salt. The average person consumes twenty times more sodium than the body needs.
6. Aim for your proper body weight. As a rule, overweight people die before those who maintain a proper body weight.

These suggestions apply to everyone but especially to those who view the body as God's dwelling place. Eating right is wisc temple keeping.

WALK FOR YOUR LIFE

The story is told of two farmers out for a morning walk when suddenly a black bear appeared behind them. One farmer quickly sat down and put on his running shoes. The other farmer laughed at him and mocked, "You can't outrun that bear!" "No," answered the other farmer, "but I can outrun you!"

Webster defines *exercise* as "bodily exertion for keeping the organs and functions healthy." In 1996, the Surgeon General included inactivity as a risk factor for premature death and disability.

The fact is, exercise slows time down. Seniors need to be encouraged and even pushed to exercise as much as possible.

According to Donald H. Kausler and Barry C. Kausler, "Millions of older men won't eat vegetables, won't exercise, and won't participate in a senior health promotion program. Nor do older men visit a physician as often as older women do. When they do see a physician, they ask fewer questions and seek less information than older women do. Many older men see themselves as being self-reliant. Seeing a physician may be viewed as a sign of weakness."[5]

Moderate exercise can produce dramatic results in overall good health. Mayo Clinic has prepared a booklet titled *Walk Your Way to Fitness,* which states, "A brisk walk, thirty to sixty minutes each day, can help you live a longer, healthier life. . . . Exercise doesn't have to be a high-intensity activity. Even walking slowly can lower your risk of heart disease. Walking faster, farther, and more frequently offers even greater health benefits."

My wife and I are avid walkers. On excessively hot or stormy days, we walk at a mall before the shoppers arrive. After thirty or forty minutes, we sit for a casual glass of juice or a fruit cup. We began several decades ago and attempt to walk a minimum of two miles per day, four or five days a week. I began walking as a stress reliever and found it helped me cope with the pressures of work. Walking also enhances sleep. In fact, if I do not walk or work in the garden, my sleep is significantly impaired. Walking for me is the key to every other activity; however, it requires discipline.

Walking also sharpens and stimulates the mind. Some of my best ideas for writing and speaking have come to me as I walked. Frankly, I can't afford not to walk. I walk for my life. For me, walking is a part of temple keeping. I walk to honor God.

EMOTIONS

Worry, fear, and depression are emotions common to all. General Ulysses S. Grant tells in his memoirs how he had become dizzy and could not see well because of violent headaches. His entire body ached. The following morning a horseman galloped up to him with a note of surrender from General Robert E. Lee of the Confederate army. Grant said, "I was instantly cured when I saw the contents of the note. Every pain immediately left me; even my headache." Grant had been sick from worry.

In spring 1871, a young man picked up a book and read twenty-one words that changed his life. The young man was a medical student at the Montreal General Hospital. He was worried about final examinations. Larger worries also bothered him. He was troubled about what he should do with his life, where he should establish his medical practice, and how he would build it.

The twenty-one words that changed his life were written by Thomas Carlyle. The man who was challenged was William Osler, a founder of Johns Hopkins School of Medicine. Here are the twenty-one words:

> *Our main business is not to see*
> *What lies dimly at a distance but*
> *To do what lies clearly at hand.*[6]

This idea is taught in the Lord's Prayer. "Give us *this day* our daily bread" (Matthew 6:11, italics added). Notice the words "this day." The prayer asks for today's bread only. It does not complain about yesterday's bread; nor does it worry about the bread for the next week or next month. The focus is on "this day." Worry doesn't solve tomorrow's problems, but it does ruin today's happiness.

Today's bread is the only bread we can eat. This is what Matthew 6:34 states: "Do not worry about tomorrow, for tomorrow will worry about itself. Each day has enough trouble of its own" (NIV).

Stress winds us up and also wears us down. "Died of worry"

could be written on thousands of tombstones. Worry leads to loss of power to will. When we worry, we become so divided that it is difficult to act in a single direction or even make the smallest decision.

Unfortunately, worry is a leading ailment in our world, and it's contagious. Charles Haddon Spurgeon, a nineteenth-century London minister, relates how he worried for weeks before a speaking engagement, even to the extent of hoping he would break a leg before the particular occasion. The result was that when it was time to speak, he was exhausted from worry.

Then Spurgeon faced up to the situation. He asked, "What is the worst thing that could happen to me during my address?" Whatever it was, he decided, the heavens would not fall. He recognized that he had been magnifying his fears. When he faced his worries for what they were, he relaxed, simply because his mind was no longer divided.

A CURE FOR WORRY

Consider Prayer

Luke 18:1 reads, "Men ought always to pray, and not to faint" (KJV). Prayer is God's cure for falling apart.

September 11, 2001, may have been one of the bloodiest days in U.S. history when two of our biggest office towers were destroyed and the Pentagon, a symbol of American military authority, was torn apart like an egg carton. In the aftermath of this attack, millions of people turned to prayer.

Alfred Tennyson wrote, "More things are wrought by prayer than this world dreams of." Prayer is the way to cope with worry.

Consider Trust

The psalmists encourage us to bring our fears to God in faith. "Trust in the Lord, and do good" (Psalm 37:3). Fear creates friction but little forward progress. Fretting heats the axle but fails to generate forward movement. Worry is a form of atheism because it closes our eyes to God's active concern and care.

Make a list of what worries you. As you list the items, you will discover many are vague and unnecessary.

Consider Work

Psalm 37 suggests, "Trust in the Lord, and *do good*" (italics added). One of the best cures for worry is *work*. "It is not work that kills men," wrote Henry Ward Beecher. "It is worry. Work is healthy. . . . Worry is rust on the blade." Work makes the day go faster. There are days when I do not feel good *until* I become involved in some project. Work is a vital part of being alive. Positive work on behalf of others is one of the best ways to overcome worry. Though we do not engage in works for God's acceptance, Scripture urges all "to be ready for every good work" (Titus 3:1).

Suppose a group of vandals broke into your local place of worship and smashed the stained glass windows, splintered the pews, and stained the carpets. You would be offended and rightly so. Desecrating a house of worship is a serious matter. Yet it is far more tragic to vandalize the human body, God's temple, through worry, unnecessary fear, inactivity, and poor eating habits. Temple keeping is strategic to successful aging.

To me, old age is fifteen years older than I am.

BERNARD BARUCH

❦

*A stock broker urged Claude Pepper to buy stock that
would triple in value every year. Pepper replied,
"At my age, I don't even buy green bananas."*

❦

*Harry Hershfield said, "I wake up every morning at 8
A.M. and reach for the morning paper. Then I look at the
obituary page.
If my name's not in it, I GET UP."*

4

❧

THE AGE BOOM

There's no doubt about it; our world is experiencing a phenomenon like no other in recorded history. Peter G. Peterson, chairman of the Blackstone Group and advisor to presidents, says, "Global aging will become the transcendent political and economic issue of the twenty-first century."[1]

Because of the advances in medicine, science, nutrition, and health awareness, most people will live longer than they expected. Retirement could well be deferred to age seventy or even eighty while others may choose to pursue new careers several times.

In the past, long life was the exception rather than the rule.

In 1776, when the United States became an independent nation, a person could expect to live about thirty-five years, even though the median age of the population was sixteen. By 1876, there was a modest improvement and life expectancy was forty, while the median age was twenty-one. The high death rate and high birthrate helped keep America young. It's interesting to visit the graves of historic cemeteries and realize many of the soldiers were between fifteen and twenty-five years of age.

The builders of the railroads and canals were also young people, often immigrants seeking a better life. My parents left Scotland for America while still in their twenties. My wife's parents likewise emigrated from Germany while still in their twenties.

CAUSE FOR THE AGE BOOM

The astounding breakthroughs in health care, along with the reduction or elimination of death-causing diseases, appear to be the major reasons for our present age boom. For example, my mother's mother died while giving birth to her third child because of a breech birth. Today, such a birth can be predicted, and both mother and child are likely to survive.

My childhood playmate's father died from tuberculosis before age thirty. Several grade school playmates died from pneumonia. My three sisters and two brothers experienced an array of childhood diseases from scarlet fever to measles. My older brother nearly died at age fourteen from a streptococcus infection. The dreaded disease of the 1930s was poliomyelitis; however, with the arrival of the Salk vaccine, this scourge has been almost eradicated. Scores of life-threatening diseases have been practically removed.

Science and medicine have added approximately twenty-eight years of life to the average person since the early 1900s. A child born today in the USA has a life expectancy of approximately seventy-five years. The National Bureau of Aging projects that by 2040 men will probably live an average of eighty-six years and women, about ninety-two years.

Many nations are building a society of active, involved, and relatively healthy seniors.

In his book *The Virtues of Aging,* former President Carter reminds us that Americans over age sixty-five outnumber teenagers. He also says that during the past twenty-four years those over eighty-five grew at a pace about six times greater than the overall population, and—get this—those over one hundred years of age are the fastest-growing group of all. In 1956, there were 2,500 centenarians, 25,000 in 1986, and about 268,000 by the year 2000. It is estimated that by the year 2050 there will be 600,000 centenarians in the United States alone. No wonder Hallmark has prepared a special line of cards for this group.

WHERE PEOPLE LIVE LONGEST

The age boom is a worldwide phenomenon with thirteen countries possibly surpassing the United States in longevity. According to the U.S. Bureau of the Census (1987), here are the twenty most longevous countries (listed by percent of population over age sixty-five):

1. Sweden 18
2. Norway 16
3. United Kingdom 15
4. Denmark 15
5. Switzerland 15

6. Austria 15
7. Germany 15
8. Belgium 14
9. Italy 14
10. Greece 14
11. Luxembourg 14
12. France 13
13. Finland 13
14. Hungary 13
15. Netherlands 12
16. Spain 12
17. United States 12
18. Ireland 12
19. Bulgaria 12
20. Portugal 12

IMPLICATIONS OF THE AGE BOOM

Peter Peterson uses startling words in his book *Gray Dawn:* "There's an iceberg ahead. It's called global aging, and it threatens to bankrupt the great powers. . . . Now is the time to ring the alarm bell. . . ."[2]

Along with seniors living longer, there is a decrease in children being born. The birthrate of families today is approximately 26 percent less than the birthrate in 1970, and a whopping 75 percent less than in 1800. This combination of a low birthrate and extended years for seniors presents serious challenges for the future.

President Carter predicts a severe crunch in Social Security, Medicare, and Medicaid by 2013 unless "basic changes are made."[3] I believe these changes will be made; however, continued thought and action must be brought to bear on these issues now.

When Social Security began in the United States in 1935, approximately 40 wage earners supported one retiree. By 1990, there were only 3.3 wage earners for each retiree. It has been predicted that by 2010 there will be only 2 workers paying for each retiree. Health care faces similar difficulties, and changes must be made for the sake of our children and grandchildren. Seniors are growing in number and using more of America's health care dollars.

The question is, "Will the seniors of America and the world use their know-how, money, maturity, and political might to face and resolve these problems?" I believe they will. The American Association of Retired People (AARP) boasts that it speaks for over thirty million seniors. Obviously, the potential of seniors for good is awesome and also urgent.

OBSTACLES AND OPPORTUNITIES

Along with the alarm bell of obstacles comes the welcome bell of opportunity calling seniors to become aware of all they can *be* and *do*.

A reservoir of talent is waiting to be enlisted. Volunteerism is not dead. It's alive in our towns, cities, and churches, waiting to be mobilized for our children and grandchildren.

Specifically, seniors have *time to give*. Eighty-five percent of seniors are reasonably healthy and able to serve. (Fewer than 5 percent of seniors live in nursing homes.) They represent a huge reservoir of time, while they themselves have a need for daily meaning and fulfillment. Seniors are also the memory of the past. They help keep history alive, connecting how things *were* with how things *are*.

Many seniors have *money to give*. Because their basic lifetime needs have been met, they are able and willing to give to causes they sincerely believe in.

Seniors have *skills to pass on*. They exemplify how to survive. They can share the dangers as well as possibilities of life. They can be teachers and role models. "Consider the years of many generations. Ask your father, and he will show you; your elders, and they will tell you" (Deuteronomy 32:7). Seniors can show and tell and be a light in the darkness. Seniors can be the historians and storytellers in the community.

Each year I visit dozens of faith-based organizations. Many are managed by talented seniors. Scores thrive with the use of senior volunteers. In fact, some organizations couldn't exist without seniors. There is an ocean of untapped seniors in our churches and society waiting to be enlisted.

The age boom is an enormous open door for seniors to serve.

You and I were created for joy and if we miss it, we miss the reason for our existence. . . . If our joy is honest joy, it must somehow be congruous with human tragedy. This is the test of joy's integrity: is it compatible with pain? . . . Only the heart that hurts has the right to joy.

LEWIS B. SMEDES

❦

Joy is not gush; joy is not jolliness. Joy is perfect acquiescence in God's will because the soul delights itself in God Himself.

H. W. WEBB-PEPLOE

❦

Joys are always on the way to us. They are always traveling to us through the darkness of the night. There is never a night when they are not coming.

AMY CARMICHAEL

❦

Enjoy the little things . . . for one day you may look back and realize . . . they were the big things.

ROBERT BRAULT

*Old age has its pleasures, which though different,
are no less than the pleasures of youth.*

W. SOMERSET MAUGHAM

*Even youths grow tired and weary, and young men stumble
and fall; but those who hope in the LORD will renew their
strength. They will soar on wings like eagles; they will run
and not grow weary, they will walk and not be faint.*

ISAIAH 40:30–31 (NIV)

5

AGING WITH JOY

One of the famous riddles of ancient literature is the "Riddle of the Sphinx": "What goes on four feet, then on two feet, and then on three, but the more feet it goes on, the weaker it be?" The answer is man! In childhood, he creeps on all fours. As an adult, he walks erect on two feet. In old age, he steadies himself with a cane.

All of life is a journey. We move from the helplessness of infancy to the strength of adults, and if life lasts long enough, we return to weakness and dependence again. It's possible, though, to age with joy, and that's the theme of this chapter. Thousands of people are experiencing joy during the last season of life. Joy does not mean the absence of pain or freedom from the normal effects of aging. Rather, joy is an attitude that evolves out of trust . . . that God is in charge. Of course, most agree that old age comes too fast. As my German father-in-law used to say, "Too soon old, too late smart." Frankly, I'm shocked at the brevity of life.

In *To the Good Long Life,* Morton Puner quotes the British writer J. B. Priestly. When asked, at age seventy-nine, what it's like to be old, Priestly answered, "It's as though I was walking down Shaftsburg Avenue as a fairly young man, and I was suddenly kidnapped, rushed into a theater and made to don the gray hair, the wrinkles and other marks of age—then wheeled on stage. Yet behind the appearance of age, I'm still the very same person with the same thoughts as when I was younger."[1]

At age seventy-eight, I agree with Priestly. Though I bear the marks of aging, I still think like I did in my forties and fifties. At times, I even plan that way and then panic when I can't do what my mind has agreed to do.

CHALLENGE AND CHANGE

Aging forces changes. The later years are times when most people cut back from earlier occupations to allow for more leisure and personal pursuits. Younger minds and hands take up the tasks that once were ours.

As we age, we're forced to find new roles to fill. I have enjoyed preparing others to take over and have reveled in their success. As we age, we discover slowly but surely that our strength and energy decrease. Often we experience a reluctance to act decisively; although we are present and involved, a detachment begins to evolve.

Overcoming a Negative Outlook

Society and science historically have promoted a negative view of aging. William Shakespeare showed his bias when he wrote,

> *Crabbed age and youth cannot live together:*
> *Youth is full of pleasance, age is full of care;*
> *Youth, like summer morn, age like winter weather;*
> *Youth, like summer brave, age like winter bare.*
> *Youth is full of sport, age's breath is short;*
> *Youth is nimble, age is lame;*
> *Youth is hot and bold, age is weak and cold;*
> *Youth is wild, and age is tame;*
> *Age, I do abhor thee, youth I do adore thee.*

FROM "THE PASSIONATE PILGRIM," 1590

At first glance, even the Bible seems to suggest that the closing years of life are tough. "Remember now your Creator in the days of your youth, before *the difficult days come,* and the years draw near when you say, 'I have no pleasure in them'" (Ecclesiastes 12:1, italics added). That's a depressing picture painted by Solomon. One translation calls the last days of life "evil days" (NASB).

Solomon adds details that are the pits. He describes the bodily decay of growing older. The "keepers of the house" (the arms and hands) begin to tremble. The "strong men" (limbs and feet) will "bow down" as they grow more feeble. The "grinders" (teeth) will "cease because they are few." The passage goes on to say, "And those that look through the windows" (eyes) will be dimmed by advancing years. And the inescapable end . . . is death (verses 3, 5).

However, there are advantages to aging.

1. Most of life's struggles are past.
2. Your secrets are safe with your friends . . . because they can't remember them either.
3. There's very little left to learn . . . the hard way.
4. Kidnappers are not interested in you.
5. You can have a big party, and the neighbors don't even realize it.
6. You can get into a heated argument over pension plans.
7. You can eat dinner at 4:30 P.M.
8. You quit trying to hold your stomach in.
9. Your investment into health insurance is finally paying off.
10. Your joints are more accurate than the weather service.

However, for those of faith, age has a purpose—and even *joy*.

RETIREMENT

One of the joys of aging is more leisure time. We find release from the obligations of daily work. I enjoy listening to the morning traffic report while occassionally catching a few more winks. Though retirement offers unique joys, we need to ward off a retirement mentality. I prefer to think of the senior years as a time of special service. Former President Jimmy Carter and his wife Rosalynn are choice role models as they are actively involved in major and minor ways to help people. At times, this

includes serving abroad or working with Habitat for Humanity constructing homes for the needy or doing service in their local church.

Don and Naomi Cole, though in their late seventies, have returned several times to Angola, Africa, to share with families and churches they served thirty years earlier as missionaries. Retirement is a marvelous chance to match your talents with your passions . . . in service to others.

My personal retirement, at age seventy-five, was so gradual as to be painless, allowing me to pursue my passions, only at my own pace. To suddenly retire with no plans for a meaningful use of time can be devastating. Retirement must be wisely planned.

Another great joy is to enter into the lives of our children and grandchildren. I can verify that there is no joy quite like watching grandchildren grow. I'm a happy member of the SOGPPIP (Silly Old Grand Parents Pictures in Pocket).

We do our best to celebrate each of their birthdays with a phone call followed by breakfast or lunch at a convenient time. Since four grandchildren live a thousand miles away, we schedule their birthday event when we visit. We have rarely missed celebrating with each grandchild, and our oldest is now a twenty-five-year-old police officer.

We have three picnics a year with twenty to thirty others, and the grandchildren rarely miss. Each grandchild has a key to our home, and knows, come what may, we are there for them.

GROWTH

Our senior years should also be a time of *growth*. Anyone who stops growing is old whether he's eighteen or eighty. The apostle Paul was told that suffering was to be part of his future,

yet as he says farewell to the elders of the church of Ephesus he tells them: "None of these things move me; nor do I count my life dear to myself, so that I may finish my race *with joy*" (Acts 20:24, italics added). It is possible to age . . . with joy.

Our last years give us a chance to live out God's will . . . *with joy!* I like to remember that when Paul made this statement he had no idea what was in his future. Yet he was willing to give God a blank check and let Him fill it in. He was a growing person.

Each of us is invited to do the same with our senior years. We can say, "I want to finish my days *with grace and joy*."

Retirement offers the chance to refine our character. Like the burning bush that drew Moses in the wilderness, God may want to make your life a bright light to glow in the darkness, that will in turn encourage others along the way.

Psalm 71 is called the psalm for seniors. The psalmist voices some of the feelings that accompany aging but also states his strong desire to be *a light* in the darkness: "Since my youth . . . you have taught me, and to this day I declare your marvelous deeds. Even when I am old and gray, do not forsake me, O God, *till I declare your power* to the next generation, your might to all who are to come" (verses 17–18 NIV, italics added).

Each senior has the privilege—and I might add the responsibility—of sharing God's ways with the next generation. Our senior years need not be pointless, but rather joyful, as we pass the torch to others. Like Caleb we say, "Give me this mountain" as a legacy to our grandchildren and great-grandchildren.

BUILDING THE INNER LIFE

Early in life, I came to the conclusion that the inner life was of lasting importance. During college days, I asked questions

like, "Why am I here? What is my reason for existing?" Slowly but surely, I realized my outer life was temporal, fragile, and transitory. By contrast, the inner life, though unseen, offered enormous possibilities. The physical life inevitably declines—whereas the inner life can continue to grow.

Retirement offers a unique opportunity to focus on the inside. Saint Paul said it this way: "We do not lose heart. Even though our outward man is perishing, yet the *inward man* is being renewed day by day" (2 Corinthians 4:16, italics added).

Many years ago while vacationing on the New Jersey shore, I read an unforgettable sentence from Anne Morrow Lindbergh's book, *Gift from the Sea*. She writes, "Simplification of the outward life is not enough. It is merely the outside. But I am starting with the outside. I am looking at the outside of a shell, the outside of my life—the shell. The complete answer is not to be found on the outside, in an outward mode of living. This is only a technique, a road to grace. The final answer, I know, is always inside."[2]

"The final answer . . . is always inside." Regardless of age, there are things we can do *now* to encourage the inside.

First, we need to become aware that there is an inner life, and it needs to be nurtured. Despite the hectic demands of daily life, only that which is eternal ultimately matters. In my first year of college, I read *Practicing the Presence of God* by Brother Lawrence. I resolved to consciously and subconsciously seek God's presence in the ordinary chores of everyday living.

Retirement is an invitation to focus on the inside. Blaise Pascal said, "All men's miseries derive from not being able to sit quiet in a room *alone*." Rather than being discouraged because of physical decline, we can focus on "the inside."

Second, I made a conscious effort to pursue the reading of

great books. Nothing refreshes me like a book. Through reading, we can travel the world and listen to the brightest and the best. Through reading, pain will lessen, and we're able to rise above the nagging irritations of daily situations. I cannot overemphasize the importance of feeding and stimulating the mind and heart. A sincere thirst to grow is a vital ingredient to joyful aging.

For me, several chapters of the Bible a day lift my spirit and feed my soul. This, coupled with quietness, study, and prayer, is life building. My goal is to renew "the inside."

Third, I faithfully pursue corporate as well as individual worship, to encourage "the inside." Worship is the communion of our souls with God. It means rubbing our cold, weary lives against the beauty of His holiness. Scripture reminds us *not* to forsake "the assembling of ourselves together" (Hebrews 10:25). Corporate worship invigorates "the inside."

However, corporate worship needs to be undergirded by individual worship. Sometimes we refer to this as *devotions* or *quiet time.* Whatever the name, it is that time each day when we give ourselves to God—to reacknowledge His lordship.

The Psalms have been life-giving to me. During two surgeries, I peacefully went into surgery quoting, "The Lord is the strength of my life; of whom shall I be afraid?" (Psalm 27:1).

Several years ago, while vacationing at the ocean, I walked the sandy beach with my then four-year-old granddaughter, Katie. After walking a considerable distance, she tired and asked me to carry her. However I too was struggling with the soft sand and the slope of the beach and told my granddaughter I was unable to carry her. She looked up at me, as only a four-year-old granddaughter can do, and said, "Grandpa, if you carry me *now* . . . when you're old and little, I will carry you." Wow!

Whereupon, I received an infusion of supernatural strength, swept her into my arms, and carried her all the way home with joy.

Later that day, I shared this experience with my wife. She exclaimed, "That's Isaiah 46:4: 'Even to your old age and gray hairs I am he, I am he who will sustain you. I have made you and *I will carry you*'" (NIV, italics aded). Both of us read that verse several times and claimed it as a promise for our senior years.

Yes, you can age . . . with joy!

A SEVENTEENTH-CENTURY NUN'S PRAYER

Lord, Thou knowest better than myself
Know that I am growing older and will someday be old.
Keep me from the fatal habit of thinking I must say
something on every subject and on every occasion.
Release me from the craving to straighten out everybody's affairs.
Make me thoughtful, but not moody; helpful, but not bossy.

With my vast store of wisdom it seems a pity not to use it all,
But Thou knowest, O Lord, that I want a few friends at the end.
Keep my mind free from the recital of endless details;
Give me wings to get to the point,
Seal my lips on my aches and pains,
They are increasing, and love of rehearsing
them is becoming sweeter as the days go by.

I dare not ask for grace enough to enjoy the tales of others' pains,
But help me to endure them with patience.
I dare not ask for an improved memory,
But for a growing humility and a lessening cocksureness
when my memory seems to clash with the memories of others.
Teach me the glorious lesson that occasionally I may be mistaken.

Keep me reasonably sweet; I do not want to be a saint;
Some of them are so hard to live with—
But a sour old person is one of the crowning works of the devil.
Give me the ability to see good things in unexpected places,
and talents in unexpected people.
And give me, O Lord, the grace to tell them so.
Amen.

When writer Somerset Maugham was recuperating
from the flu, an admirer called and asked,
"Could I send you fruit or would you prefer flowers?"
He was eighty-eight years old. He told her,
"It's too late for fruit, and too early for flowers."

W. SOMERSET MAUGHAM

I married an archaeologist because the older I grow,
the more he appreciates me.

AGATHA CHRISTIE

Because you have an occasional spell of despondency,
do not despair. After all, remember that the sun has a
sinking spell every night but rises again in the morning.

UNKNOWN

For age is opportunity no less than youth itself,
tho' in another dress. And as the evening twilight fades
away, the sky is filled with stars . . . invisible by day.

HENRY WADSWORTH LONGFELLOW

gin. Exercise and the ability to avoid stress are two ways to improve arterial health. Careless living and inactivity ages the cardiovascular system more quickly. Poor food choices result in added weight, and added weight hinders exercise. Arterial health is something to strive after.

Though the emphasis of this chapter concerns a person's attitude, always remember that healthy arteries are an important key to successful aging.

ATTITUDES ARE IMPORTANT

Because each person is unique, attitudes vary greatly. Some face aging pessimistically and appear to increase the difficulties of life while others take a more positive view.

Victor S. Frankl tells of his experiences in a concentration camp during World War II: "We who lived in the concentration camps can remember the men who walked through the huts comforting others, giving away their last piece of bread. They may have been few in number, but they offer sufficient proof that everything can be taken from a man but one thing, the last of his freedoms—to choose one's attitudes in any given set of circumstances, to choose one's own way."

To choose your attitude toward aging is a mind-stretching challenge and just might be life extending. I heard Clement Stone say, "There is little difference in people, but that little difference makes a big difference. That little difference is attitude."

Experts in aging make a distinction between passive aging and purposeful aging. Successful, purposeful aging calls for continued involvement, relationships, discipline, and an attitude of faith.

Three old-timers were playing a round of golf. One complained about the oppressive humidity. The other griped about

6

ARTERIES
PLUS ATTITUDE

Recently I read a book that included a chapter titled, "Attitudes, Not Arteries." The author was helpful; however, the title suggested a person's arteries are unimportant. Nothing could be further from the truth.

After consulting with several doctors, I am convinced that nothing keeps a person healthier than keeping the cardiovascular system healthy. Research affirms that more people die from cardiovascular disease than from any other cause. Michael F. Roizen, M.D., reminds us in his book *Real Age* our "arteries are like streets that eventually wear out. They become blocked with a substance called plaque. As the arteries grow older and clogged they are subject to clots."[1]

What can we do to prevent arterial aging? We can eat right. A diet low in saturated fat is the place to be-the roughness of the greens. The third was more optimistic and quipped, "At least we're on the right side of the grass."

Michael DeSaint-Pierre comments, "An optimist may see a light where there is none, but why must the pessimist always run to blow it out? When two pessimists meet, they don't shake hands . . . they shake heads."

A story is told of a duck hunter and his sensational dog. Whenever he shot a flying duck, his dog would run *on top of the water* and retrieve the duck. However, his hunting buddies never appeared to notice or comment about this extraordinary dog. On one occasion, after downing several ducks, he could no longer stand their silence and asked directly, "Didn't you notice anything unusual about my hunting dog?" To which they responded, "Yes, he can't swim!"

IT'S NATURAL TO BE NEGATIVE

It's easy and natural to be negative in life. Contrary to the views of some, I believe there is a place for negative thinking. Some things are always wrong and must be recognized as harmful. For example, the Ten Commandments call attention to several negative acts: "You shall *not* murder. You shall *not* commit adultery. You shall *not* steal" (Exodus 20:13–15, italics added). The apostle Paul wrote that creation groans because of the fall of man (Romans 8:22). The voice of nature, whether it's the wind, waves, beasts of the field, or birds of the air, is heard in the minor key. All of creation groans. Paul goes on to say, "*We also* who have the firstfruits of the Spirit . . . groan within ourselves . . . waiting for . . . the redemption of our body" (Romans 8:23, italics added). Groaning is normal, and even natural.

I must confess occasionally I groan while on my daily walks. When my wife chides me for my groaning, I remind her with a smile that *"groaning is biblical."* However, Paul speaks of a day when our natures will be changed from discord to harmony and from imperfection to perfection. Then we will have ageless bodies, and we will groan no more.

Paul continues to tell how we can encourage an attitude of joy . . . *now*, in this life, if we choose.

AN ATTITUDE OF JOY

While in a Roman jail, Paul illustrates an attitude of joy. He said, "The things which happened to me have actually turned out for the furtherance of the gospel" (Philippians 1:12).

Conceivably, Paul could have groaned about his imprisonment and written:

Dear Friends,

I have discovered that it really doesn't pay to serve God. Notice where I am: in jail, and I don't like it one bit. To think I've been faithful all these years, and I end up in prison. I'm disappointed, bitter, and resentful.

Unhappily yours, the apostle Paul

By contrast, consider this expanded paraphrase (Philippians 1:12–14):

Dear Friends,

I want you to know this is the first time I've ever had a mission tour paid for by the Roman government. But more than that, they chain soldiers to me for twenty-four hours a day; and

I share with them. Every eight hours, they change the guards, and I have a new congregation. Some are coming to faith in Caesar's palace. I'm having a ball. Wish you were here. Keep up the support.

Joyfully yours, the apostle Paul

Possibly, you're thinking, *How can I acquire a believing attitude in a negative world?* Paul suggests two ways. "If God is for us, who can be against us?" (Romans 8:31). This could be paraphrased, "Since God is for us, it doesn't really matter who's against us." He reminds his audience that God is not neutral about His own but is enthusiastically *for us.* That's mind stretching.

There are times in life when we're not for ourselves, yet God is *for* us, *with* us, *helping* us, and *cheering* us on. The knowledge that God is inclined toward us is good news in a challenging world.

The following verse offers an even greater promise, assuring us that "He who did not spare His own Son, but delivered Him up for us all, how shall He not with Him also *freely give us all things?*" (verse 32, italics added). Or . . . every conceivable thing I need to *survive* and *thrive.*

An Attitude of Thanks

I'm invited, by prayer and supplication, with thanksgiving, to let my requests be made known to God (Philippians 4:6).

It's easy to be thankful when life flows along like a song— when the sky is blue, the sun shines brightly, and the gentle breezes blow. But what about those times when health wanes and money is scarce? Can we be thankful then?

The psalmist wrote, "Many . . . are Your wonderful works . . . and Your thoughts toward us . . . they are more than can be numbered" (Psalm 40:5).

The influence of a grateful spirit is hard to exaggerate. An attitude of thankfulness encourages a feeling of well-being. Occasionally, I number the things for which I'm thankful. For example:

1. Faith in a caring heavenly Father
2. The love of family and friends
3. Health that is reasonably good
4. The challenge and enjoyment of work
5. The privilege of contributing to the lives of others
6. The ability to meet my financial obligations
7. A good night's sleep
8. Waking up to the smell of coffee and burnt toast (I like burnt toast.)
9. More than my daily bread to eat
10. A daily walk with my wife and a little more coffee
11. The privilege of taking our ten grandchildren out to breakfast one at a time, and learning their likes and dislikes
12. Fellowship and inspiration with the people of our local church
13. Finding a parking place, especially when I'm late
14. Laughing enthusiastically until it hurts
15. An occasional afternoon nap—"nature's sweet restorative"
16. Pruning roses in our garden or picking berries
17. Reading a good book
18. Listening to old songs and remembering when . . .

19. Watching the sun rise and set
20. The sound of rain beating on the windowpane
21. Chatting with neighbors about small things

Especially, I'm thankful for the privilege of *prayer*. That in all the experiences of life I'm invited, "by prayer and supplication, with *thanksgiving*, [to] let [my] requests be made known to God" (Philippians 4:6, italics added).

The worst moment for an atheist must be when he's really thankful and has no one to thank. Clean arteries plus an attitude of joy and thanks are important to successful aging, and each involves a conscious choice.

If I can make people smile,
then I have served my purpose for God.

COMEDIAN RED SKELTON

You can turn painful situations around through laughter.
If you can find humor in anything—
even in poverty—you can survive it.

COMEDIAN BILL COSBY

Ten minutes of genuine belly laughter
had an anesthetic effect and would give me
at least two hours of pain-free sleep.

NORMAN COUSINS

I have seen what a laugh can do. It can transform almost
unbearable tears into something bearable—even hopeful.

COMEDIAN BOB HOPE

Laughter is a form of internal jogging.

NORMAN COUSINS

It is bad to suppress laughter.
It goes back down and spreads your hips.

COMEDIAN FRED ALLEN

It is pleasing to the dear God whenever thou rejoicest
or laughest from the bottom of thy heart.

MARTIN LUTHER

Humor opposes directly those emotions which have been
specifically recorded as being associated with precipitation
of heart attack. These emotions are fear and rage.
Humor acts to relieve fear.
Rage is impossible when mirth prevails.

DR. WILLIAM F. FRY JR.

We have a lot of evidence that shows mirth and laughter
affect most of the major physical systems of the body.

DR. WILLIAM F. FRY JR.

Like a welcome summer rain, humor may suddenly
cleanse and cool the earth, the air, and you.

LANGSTON HUGHES

*If you wish to glimpse inside a human soul and get to
know a man, don't bother analyzing his ways of
being silent, of talking, of weeping, of seeing
how much he is moved by noble ideas; you will get better
results if you just watch him laugh.
If he laughs well, he's a good man.*

FYODOR DOSTOYEVSKY

*Being 80 is a lot better than being 70. At 70, people are
mad at you for everything. At 80, you have a perfect excuse
no matter what you do. If you act foolishly,
it's your second childhood. Everybody is looking
for symptoms of softening of the brain.*

FRANK C. LAUBACH

*Old age is when you get out of the shower
and you're glad the mirror is all fogged up.*

*The seven ages of man: spills, drills,
thrills, bills, ills, pills, wills.*

RICHARD NEEDHAM

Old age: When actions creak louder than words.

DANA ROBBINS

A person without a sense of humor is like a wagon without springs—jolted by every pebble in the road.

HENRY WARD BEECHER

7

WHY COMEDIANS
LIVE SO LONG

Before this chapter is finished, I believe you will have the answer to the question, "Why do comedians live so long?" Of course, I cannot prove it, but there appears to be a positive relationship between humor and longevity. At least a sense of humor helps to cope with the stresses of life and just might have life-extending value. Comedians give their lives to help people laugh and, in return, appear to benefit by extra years.

LAUGHTER REDUCES STRESS

George Vaillant, in his studies of a large group of male Harvard graduates, "consistently found that a sense of humor is associated not only with good physical health, but also with superior psychological adjustment." Vaillant considers humor to be the best coping mechanism available to us. He goes on to say, "We use humor both to recognize hard realities and protect ourselves from their inherent sorrow and hurt."[1]

Laughter has been called "the safety valve of the nervous system," and I might add . . . so are tears. However, tears are draining and sloppy. Laughter relaxes our body much like ordinary exercise.

William Fry, a researcher from Stanford University, believes that laughter increases disease-fighting antibodies into the bloodstream, enabling the body to ward off infection.

Decades ago, Jonathan Swift wrote, "The best doctors in the world are Dr. Diet, Dr. Quiet, and Dr. Merryman." The word *merry* means full of laughter, lively, cheerful. Thousands of years ago, Solomon wrote, "Pleasant words are like a honeycomb, sweetness to the soul and health to the bones" (Proverbs 16:24). Are pleasant words sweet? Can laughter bring health to our bones? Solomon also said, "A merry heart makes a cheerful countenance, but by sorrow of the heart the spirit is broken" (Proverbs 15:13). There's no doubt about it: Cheerful people look better.

While I was recovering from prostate surgery, a friend sent me a card with this verse: "A merry heart does good, like medicine, but a broken spirit dries the bones" (Proverbs 17:22). Is laughter good, like medicine? Is a gloomy spirit life draining? My surgeon felt the answer was yes, in both cases.

In most books on aging, humor is high on the list of things that contribute to a sense of enjoyment and longevity. So learn to laugh . . . it's good for you.

LAUGHTER IS THERAPEUTIC

Executive Digest states:

> Scientists have been studying the effect of laughter on human beings and have found that laughter has a profound and instantaneous effect on virtually every important organ in the human body. Laughter reduces health-sapping tensions and relaxes the tissues as well as exercising the most vital organs. It is said that laughter, even when forced, results in beneficial effects mentally and physically. Next time you feel nervous and jittery, *indulge in a good laugh.*[2] (italics added)

Occasionally, someone will tell me he has nothing in life to laugh about. I urge him to try to laugh anyway. Even forced laughter can be helpful. Laughter *is* good medicine.

I recall a service in one of my pastorates when the choirmaster introduced the handbell choir. Inadvertently, he said, "And now . . . the Hand*ball* Choir." We enjoyed a good laugh.

On another occasion, the church sanctuary was filled with four thousand people waiting for a concert to begin. The program was to be broadcast. When it was time to begin, the engineer from the sound room pointed to the conductor to begin, but the conductor didn't respond. Unaware that the microphones were open, the engineer blurted out for all to hear— like a voice from heaven, "Tell the old goat to get the show on the road." A startled audience broke into laughter.

Laughter is good medicine (Proverbs 17:22). Laughter is exercise. Can you ever remember laughing 'til it hurt? . . . 'til you became light-headed?

Norman Cousins, onetime editor of *The Saturday Review*, was told at age thirty-nine that he had three months to live. After reading about the relationship of stress to health, he determined to pursue laughter as a stress reducer. He began a daily routine of watching humorous films or TV programs like *Candid Camera*, Abbott and Costello, *I Love Lucy*, and *The Honeymooners*. He read upbeat stories and literature of a humorous, uplifting nature.

Not only did he find relief from pain, but he lived an additional thirty-nine years (dying in 1990 at age seventy-eight). He also became adjunct professor in the Department of Behavioral Medicine at the University of California, Los Angeles School of Medicine.

Pleasant words do, indeed, appear to be health building. Laughter is the best medicine available, and it's hard to overdose!

DOES GOD HAVE A SENSE OF HUMOR?

Of all the creatures created by God, only man has the ability to laugh. Recently, I was asked at a seminar if God had a sense of humor.

Ecclesiastes 3:4 tells us there is "a time to laugh." The psalmist also speaks of God laughing at the presumption of rebellious people (Psalm 2:4). Because all people are made in God's likeness—and we have a sense of humor—it seems logical that God has a sense of humor, too.

When Abraham at age one hundred and his wife, Sarah, at age ninety were told they would have a son, Sarah said, "God made me laugh, and all who hear will laugh with me (Genesis 21:6). They named their miracle baby, Isaac, which means "to laugh."

Occasionally, I have smiled while reading Paul's letter to Timothy, "Alexander the coppersmith did me much harm. May the Lord repay him according to his works" (2 Timothy 4:14).

Abraham Lincoln said, "God must have meant us to laugh, else He would not have made so many mules, parrots, monkeys . . . and human beings."

The older I get, the more I enjoy people-watching—it's hilarious! And I know that people are laughing at me as well.

Helen Salsbury wrote,

> *Dear God, we make You so solemn,*
> *So stiff and staid—*
> *How can we be so foolish*
> *When we look at the things You've made?*

> *How can we miss the twinkle,*
> *That must have been in Your eye,*
> *When You planned the hippopotami*
> *And the rhinoceri?*

> *Who watches an ostrich swallow,*
> *Then doubts that You like to play,*
> *Or questions Your sense of humor,*
> *Hearing a donkey bray?*

> *Could the God who made the monkey*
> *Have forgotten how to laugh—*
> *Or the One who striped the zebra*
> *And stretched out the giraffe?*

How could a solemn God
Fashion a pelican—
Or a perfectly somber Creator
Ever imagine man?[3]

Someone may respond that someday we will give account for idle words (Matthew 12:36). Les Flynn writes, "Humorous words are not necessarily idle words, any more than some serious words. Idle words are those *without a purpose*. Since the purpose of words is to carry on the business of life, encourage others, and refresh the minds, any word designed to bring relief from the . . . monotonous pressures of life is not idle."[4]

Faith does not oppose humor, rather it opposes the abuse of humor. Humor is part of life. Humor that is hurtful or sordid is offensive and dangerous, but good humor is a special gift from God.

Les Flynn writes, "Laughing can be as spiritual as singing or crying. A moderate . . . use of our sense of humor is not incompatible with joy."[5]

A reporter interviewed a man on his 100th birthday. "Tell me, sir, to what do you attribute your longevity?" The oldster replied, "To the fact that I was born . . . a long, long time ago."

"To what do you attribute your long life?" the reporter asked a man who was celebrating his 107th birthday. "Don't know for sure yet," said the old-timer. "My lawyer's negotiating with two breakfast-food companies."

On one of his rare trips to the city, Grandpa was so fascinated by a large building's elevator that he stood in front of one for several minutes. He watched an old lady, bent and wrinkled, enter. He saw the door close and she was gone. Moments later, he watched amazed as the same door opened and out stepped an attractive young lady. Grandpa rushed for the door shouting, "I'm gonna bring Grandma here!"

A reporter was interviewing three wrinkle-faced codgers on a park bench. He asked the first, "What do you do for amusement, and how old are you?" He answered, "I play checkers, and I am ninety-eight." To the same question, the second old man replied, "I play chess, and I am ninety-five." And the third replied, "I drink alcohol every day, smoke ten cigars, and stay up all night." "Your age?" the reporter asked. "Twenty-nine."

The reporter interviewed a woman who was celebrating her 100th birthday. "How do you do it?" he asked. "Well," she said, "I never rocked any of our twelve children to sleep. I never got up with them nights. I never washed dishes or cleaned the house. My dear husband Henry did that. May he rest in peace; he died at forty-nine."

From a lifetime of much joy and also sorrow, I can attest to the truth of Proverbs 16:24: "Pleasant words are like a honeycomb, sweetness to the soul and *health to the bones*" (italics added). Those who learn to laugh . . . *last!*

*Faith is a . . . form of knowledge
which transcends the intellect.*

MALCOLM MUGGERIDGE

❧

*Faith is a reasoning trust,
a trust which reckons thoughtfully
and confidently upon the trustworthiness of God.*

JOHN STOTT

8

❦

THE CALEB SECRET

By any standard, Caleb of the Old Testament lived a long, successful life. Even a casual review of his life reveals three longevity traits. First, Caleb was famous for his faith. He was an eighty-five-year-old optimist. Second, he kept fully involved in a giant cause for a lifetime. Third, he was connected to an extended family, tribe, and nation.

This chapter highlights Caleb's contagious faith. We first met Caleb when twelve representatives of the twelve tribes were chosen to spy out the land of Canaan (Numbers 13:2). Leaders were selected from each tribe for this strategic assignment. Caleb was chosen to represent the largest and most important tribe of Judah (Numbers 13:6). His selection speaks volumes concerning his ability and dedication.

The children of Israel had been in bondage in Egypt for more than four hundred years. Then Moses led them out through the Red Sea and across the wilderness. Finally, more than a million Israelites arrived at the border town of Kadesh Barnea. With the Promised Land before them, they could either occupy it in faith or retreat in unbelief.

After a forty-day search of the land, the twelve spies returned with their findings.

THE MAJORITY REPORT

All twelve leaders agreed the land was special. They said it flowed with milk and honey. But ten reported, "*Nevertheless* the *people* who dwell in the land are *strong;* the cities are fortified and very large; *moreover* we saw the descendants of Anak there" (Numbers 13:28, italics added). The majority report of the ten turned on two well-worked words of doubt and defeat ... *nevertheless* and *moreover.* The challenge is appealing; nevertheless, the difficulties are great; moreover ...

There was an element of truth in what they said. The cities would not surrender without a tough fight, and the Anaks were big. However, in their fear, they *magnified* the problems.

Pandemonium broke loose, and the people "wept that night" (Numbers 14:1). The negative attitude of the ten spies spread like a wildfire engulfing the whole nation. However, there were two other voices yet to be heard.

THE MINORITY REPORT

Ten spies brought back a pessimistic story. But Caleb and Joshua possessed an amazing faith. They challenged the people,

"Let us go up at once and take possession, for we are well able to overcome it" (Numbers 13:30).

Why the difference? The ten and the two were describing the same situation. The difference was that Caleb and Joshua included God in the picture. They said, "If the Lord delights in us, that's what really matters." In the light of God's ability, the difficulties melted to a reasonable size.

Caleb and Joshua focused on divine ability, while the ten looked at the land and its inhabitants. Their reports were totally different because their attitudes were totally different.

It was not just the walled cities that made the spies throw up their hands. It was not even their enemies' stature and strength. It was the spies' faulty relationship. "They have not wholly followed Me" (Numbers 32:11). They had no heart to follow. What they *were* not, determined what they *did* not.

Their separation from God first affected *their attitude toward the land*. We're told, they "have despised [it]" and brought "up a slander upon" it (Numbers 14:31, 36 KJV).

Their lack of faith also determined *their attitude toward the people*. Because the ten spies could not see God, they saw giants. Panic overwhelmed them, and fear snuffed out whatever faith they had. It's also revealing to see how their faithless attitude twisted the way they saw themselves, "There we saw the giants (the descendants of Anak came from the giants)"; they told the people, "and we were like grasshoppers in our own sight, and so we were in their sight" (Numbers 13:33).

They saw themselves as grasshoppers because instead of looking to God they focused on the giants who opposed them. It's always that way when we minimize God. The obstacles seem huge.

In their own sight they were as grasshoppers, but what were

they in God's sight? They were His chosen. He had shattered Egypt for them and defeated Amalek and others who had opposed them. Every promise He had kept, but now the past was forgotten.

ATTITUDE DETERMINES ACTION

Your attitude can work against you, but Caleb's life shows how it can also work for you. That's how it was with Caleb and Joshua.

Six times in Numbers, Deuteronomy, and Joshua, we read concerning Caleb, "He wholly followed the Lord." This tells the secret of his success. What Caleb was determined what Caleb did. His attitude determined his actions!

Caleb was an overcomer, because he had committed his entire life to God. Caleb and Joshua described the land as "an exceedingly good land" (Numbers 14:7). Earlier Caleb had urged the people to "go up at once and take possession" (Numbers 13:30).

His was the reasoning of faith. God had promised the land to the people. He had said it was theirs, that He would go with them to receive it. Caleb believed. Going against the crowd took courage. A million angry people were ready to stone him. But the majority was wrong, and Caleb was right.

Notice Caleb's attitude toward the people of Canaan. True, they were like giants, but he had placed his faith in God. "They are our bread," he told his countrymen (Numbers 14:9). That sounds something like, "They're a piece of cake."

Caleb wasn't wearing rose-colored glasses. The enemies were big and tough, but beyond them, Caleb saw the supernatural. His faith was larger than his fear.

Consider Caleb's attitude toward God. "If the Lord delights in us," he said, "then He will bring us into this land" (Numbers 14:8). He knew God's promise and believed it.

God said, "Possess the land." Unbelief said, "We can't." But Caleb saw the difficulties as opportunities to display supernatural power.

Notice Caleb's attitude toward himself. His was not an arrogant stance. He did not rely on his own ability. He saw himself linked in a unique partnership. "If the Lord delights in us," he reasoned, "then we shall succeed." Caleb knew his power was not in himself.

Why was Caleb successful?

1. Caleb desired Canaan; the ten despised it.
2. Caleb sought to enter the land; the ten slandered the land.
3. Caleb had the spirit of a winner; the ten had the spirit of losers.
4. Caleb looked up at God's promise; the others looked in at themselves and around at their enemies.
5. Caleb saw God; the ten saw giants.
6. Caleb wholly followed the Lord; the ten set Him aside.

How is it with you? Do you face a crucial decision, a Kadesh Barnea that may change the course of your future? The land to claim or the giants to fight in your life may be unspectacular. It may be a difficult circumstance to accept, a work to be undertaken, a burden to be borne, a victory to be claimed.

Remember Caleb's secret. Don't be misled by circumstances or frightened by difficulties. They're not what matters. It is your *attitude* that counts.

It's always a mistake to worry about obstacles when the Omnipotent is involved. Caleb won the battles of life because he first won the battle of faith. That was Caleb's secret . . . and it can be yours.

Fear makes the wolf bigger than he is.

GERMAN PROVERB

❧

Fear knocked at the door.
Faith answered. No one was there.

❧

Good-bye, proud world! I'm going home.

RALPH WALDO EMERSON

❧

God's finger touched him, and he slept.

ALFRED, LORD TENNYSON

❧

Today I entered on my eighty-second year and found
myself just as strong to labor and as fit for any
exercise of body or mind as I was forty years ago.

JOHN WESLEY

There is a virtuous fear which is the effect of faith,
and a vicious fear which is the product of doubt. . . .
The former leads to hope as relying on God,
in Whom we believe; the latter inclines to despair,
as not relying upon God, in Whom we do not believe.
Persons of the one character fear to lose God;
those of the other character fear to find Him.

BLAISE PASCAL

9

❧

NOTHING TO FEAR . . .
BUT FEAR ITSELF

I shall always remember the words of president-elect
Franklin D. Roosevelt, March 4, 1933. Because
President Roosevelt had been paralyzed from polio
fourteen years earlier, his son James helped his father
stand to receive the oath of office. Despite the chilly
wind, the president stood hatless and coatless, seeking
to convey strength despite his personal disability.

The United States had struggled through four
years of severe depression and ached for a ray of hope.
To the thousands gathered on the Capitol steps and the
millions listening by radio, Roosevelt confidently began, "Let me assert my firm belief, that the only thing
we have to fear . . . is fear itself—nameless, unreason-
ing, unjustified terror which paralyzes the needed

efforts to convert retreat . . . into advance." His sheer faith and charisma energized the nation to overcome its fears.

Again on September 11, 2001, our nation experienced a wave of fear when the Pentagon in Washington and the Twin Towers in New York City were attacked by terrorists. On November 1, 2001, Rick Hampton wrote in *USA Today:* "Fear is a weapon. It is the knife that would sever our faith in each other, the club that would beat us into resignation, the gun that would stop us from flying. . . . Fear would make us hoard antibiotics and seek needless tests . . . it would make us shun skyscrapers . . . it would induce a national nervous breakdown. But those who study fear agree: Frightening civilians . . . is a loser's hand."[1]

Fear knows every age group. Some are afraid to go to the supermarket even in broad daylight. Others are afraid the next phone call will bring bad news concerning the children or grandchildren. Sick people are afraid of what the doctor may discover during their next checkup. And thousands more are afraid their money will run out. Fear is without doubt the enemy of every age.

Fear, like a drop of ink in a glass of water, discolors everything. Fear ties people in knots. It paralyzes thinking and acting. It can make life a living death.

Not long ago, a group of scholars expressed their thoughts about the next fifty years. One scientist predicted a person born today would live to be one hundred years old. During that time they will probably see the world run out of oil and natural gas. They will live through a period of drought and worldwide famine. They would also live through a nuclear attack that would level a major city.

What Is Fear?

Fear is a "painful emotion marked by alarm, or dread." It is a response to what we think will be unpleasant. Fear is as old as the world.

Of course, not all fear is bad. The fear that prevents a person from stepping into a busy street may save a life. The fear that keeps us from touching a high-voltage wire or driving through a stoplight is lifesaving.

Psychologists tell us four basic fears plague people:

1. The Fear of Want

It is common and even normal to indulge in the "what-if" game. "What if I get sick, and my bills exceed my ability to pay?" "What if the country goes into a depression, and the stock market fails?" Are these legitimate fears? First, these are unlikely fears. Most of what we fear never happens. Second, for the person of faith—now, brace yourself—these fears are not valid. Why? Because ultimately God is the Provider. The issue is stated clearly in the Sermon on the Mount: "If God so clothes the grass of the field, which today is, and tomorrow is thrown into the oven, will He not much more clothe you, O you of little faith?" (Matthew 6:30).

Can you believe in God's ability to supply your needs? I find great strength in the words of David, "I have been young, and now am old; yet I have not seen the righteous forsaken, nor his descendents begging bread" (Psalm 37:25). Occasionally I quote, "The Lord is my shepherd; I shall *not want*" (Psalm 23:1, italics added).

2. The Fear of Suffering

Do you fear suffering? This could be pain of body or spirit. We tend to fear sickness, sorrow, loneliness, and grief. Suffering is part of living. God doesn't shield us from suffering but rather controls it for our advantage.

A friend of mine was seriously injured in a highway accident. She spent many pain-filled months recovering. But during those months she grew more spiritually than in all her previous years. Today she looks back at her suffering as the most important and valuable experience of her lifetime. Suffering can be an opportunity to get to know God and ourselves better. Paul wrote, "My grace is sufficient for you, for my power is made perfect in weakness" (2 Corinthians 12:9 NIV).

3. The Fear of Failure

A common kind of fear is of failure. We want to be liked. We want to be accepted and included, especially if we've lost a loved one or friend and we're alone. Regarding loneliness, we need to be a friend to others rather than waiting for others to reach out to us. This requires thoughtfulness and a conscious effort to help others.

For the person of faith, the ultimate concern is to seek God's will and do it. The heroes of faith listed in Hebrews 11 were people who believed God and gave themselves to fulfill His will.

Here's a formula for overcoming the fear of failure: "Do not let this Book of the Law depart from your mouth; meditate on it day and night, so that you may be careful to do everything written in it. Then you will be prosperous and successful" (Joshua 1:8 NIV).

4. The Fear of Death

Is life harder toward the end? Not necessarily. Granted, there are at times physical limitations, but they are balanced by the luxury of free time and the chance to pursue our passions of life. The slower pace is a treat. I enjoy each day as a time to walk, visit, read, see friends, and do good for others. The last chapter of life can be like an autumn day with a full harvest and colorful leaves. There's nothing quite like a clear, fall day.

And yet some people are fearful of death. For people of faith, death is called "the valley of the shadow of death" (Psalm 23:4). The shadow of a dog can't bite. The shadow of a gun can't kill. Because of the Resurrection, death has been robbed of its sting and is just a shadow (1 Corinthians 15). "How strange this fear of death is! We are never frightened at a sunset," writes George MacDonald.

The great musician Wolfgang Mozart lived a short life, dying at age thirty-five. At age seven he sang, composed, and played the harpsichord, the organ, and the violin, winning acclaim throughout Austria. At age thirty he wrote to his father Leopold:

> Since death is the true end and purpose of our life, I have made it my business over the past few years to get to know this true, this best friend of man so well that the thought of him not only holds no terror for me, but even brings me great comfort and peace of mind. I thank my God that He has granted me the good fortune and opportunity to get to know death as the key to our true happiness. I never go to bed without reflecting on the

thought that perhaps, as young as I am, the next day I might not be alive any more. And no man who knows me will be able to say that in social intercourse I am morose or sad. For this happiness I thank every day my Creator, and with all my heart I wish this happiness for all my fellowmen.[2]

Several years ago I invited several senior leaders to Chicago to honor them for a life of outstanding service to the church and mankind. After I read a glowing tribute to Theodore Epp of Lincoln, Nebraska, he addressed our faculty and students. He began, "This is the last sermon I will ever deliver. I have come here to finish my work, where you are beginning yours." I was startled by his opening remarks, and yet I was soon caught up in his challenge. At the close, hundreds of students asked me what he meant by his opening sentence. "I don't have a clue," I answered.

At the end of the day, Dr. Epp flew to Lincoln, Nebraska, and arrived safely. The next morning he entered the hospital for a physical checkup and never left the hospital. It was indeed his last sermon. Theodore Epp lived and died by faith.

On another occasion, Herbert Lockyer, age ninety-seven, was able to come and be honored for a lifetime of speaking and writing. His mind was sharp and his voice was full, though his body bore the marks of aging. Two students assisted him to the podium. Once there, the adrenaline flowed, and he was magnificent. Coming to the close he said, "I'm not looking for the undertaker. I'm looking for the uppertaker." As he sat down next to me on the platform, he leaned over and whispered, "Did I hit the ball out of the park?" "Yes, you did. You surely did," I replied.

Though the unknown has its moments, for people of faith fear can be displaced by trust. "What time I am afraid, I will trust in thee" (Psalm 56:3 KJV).

UP-HILL

Does the road wind up-hill all the way?
Yes, to the very end.
Will the day's journey take the whole long day?
From morn to night my friend.

But is there for the night a resting-place?
A roof for when the slow dark hours begin,
May not the darkness hide it from my face?
You cannot miss that inn.

Shall I meet other wayfarers at night?
Those who have gone before.
Then must I knock, or call when just in sight?
They will not keep you standing at that door.

Shall I find comfort, travel-sore and weak?
Of labor you shall find the sum.
Will there be beds for me and all who seek?
Yea, beds for all who come.

CHRISTINA ROSSETTI[3]

Human worth does not lie in the riches or power,
but in character or goodness. . . . If people would only
begin to develop this goodness . . . give of yourself . . .
you can always give something, even if it is only
kindness. . . . No one has ever become poor from giving.

ANNE FRANK, *The Diary of Anne Frank*

❧

The only safe rule is to give more than we can spare.
Our charities should pinch and hamper us.
If we live at the same level of
affluence as other people who have our level of income,
we are probably giving away too little.

C. S. LEWIS

❧

Money reveals where our interests lie;
it can direct our attitudes;
it ever exposes us to the danger of worshiping it; and
it represents value. Money not only talks; "it screams."

LESLIE B. FLYNN

❧

God does not need our money.
But you and I need the experience of giving it.

JAMES C. DOBSON

10

DO YOUR GIVING
WHILE YOU'RE LIVING

Giving is an essential part of being alive. Dead things may accumulate but they can't grow. Only living things . . . grow.

William Gladstone, the brilliant British statesman, said concerning giving, "There is no merit in a man leaving money in his will; he has simply got to leave it. The time to administer your trust . . . is while you are still living."

King Solomon was rich beyond any of his day. Yet in death, before his body had a chance to grow cold, the family was feuding over the distribution of his assets.

Do your giving while you're living. One benefit is the chance to see firsthand the good your giving can do. To see loved ones helped is especially rewarding.

To enable struggling people to find hope provides enormous satisfaction.

THE SIN OF OLD AGE

While leading a seminar with seniors, I was asked, "What is the sin of old age?" That's a challenging question.

I began to answer by attempting to identify the primary sin of youth. I believe that the sin of youth is, "the lust of the flesh," often referred to as "sex." Sex pervades most of life from the books we read and the films we see to the selling of undergarments. Though sex appeals to all ages, it is aimed especially at youth.

During the middle years, many wrestle with the "pride of life." You can do it! Take care of yourself! Make it while you're hot; you stay cold a long time. Ego struts its stuff, while at the same time looking for security. Ego appears to be the sin of the middle years.

But what is the sin of old age? Greed. The accumulation of things. The quest for more. The push for security. Old age confuses *having* with *being*. However, what you *are* beats what you *have*, any day.

Another word for greed is "covetousness." Covetousness is an excessive desire for things. Covetousness is a megaproblem, so deceitful as to be linked with the grossest of crimes.

It was one of the first sins committed by the children of Israel when they entered the Promised Land. A man named Achan coveted silver, gold, and clothing and took it for himself despite Joshua's warning (Joshua 7).

The Ten Commandments warns against covetousness. "You shall not covet your neighbor's house. You shall not covet your neighbor's wife . . . or anything that belongs to your neighbor" (Exodus 20:17 NIV).

WHAT IS STEWARDSHIP?

Another benefit of "giving while you're living" is the opportunity to model good stewardship. A steward is one who manages the property of another. A steward lays aside all personal interest and thinks only of the welfare of the owner.

People of faith view all property as belonging to God and ourselves as administrators. As stewards we need to be wise, honest, industrious, and, most of all, faithful.

Too often assets are given to children or friends without adequate guidance. Along with our giving, we can provide wise counsel. We can even give incrementally to observe how the gift is received and used.

John Wesley had a famous saying: "Get all you can, save all you can, give all you can." Dallas Willard suggests a modification: "Get all you can; save all you can; freely use all you can within a properly disciplined spiritual life, and control all you can for the good of humankind and God's glory. Giving all you can would then naturally be a part of an overall wise stewardship."[1]

All I have, including life itself, is a trust. Stewardship goes beyond my money and includes my body, mind, time, words, and deeds. Every person is a steward—whether he chooses to be or not. We are either good stewards or bad ones, but we cannot escape being one.

John D. Rockefeller Jr., businessman and philanthropist, said, "Giving is the secret to a healthy life. Not necessarily money, but whatever a person has to give of encouragement, sympathy, and understanding."

An ancient proverb reminds us:

> *What I kept, I lost,*
> *What I spent, I once had,*
> *What I gave, I STILL have.*

John Bunyan wrote in *The Pilgrim's Progress:* "A man there was, and they called him mad; the more he gave, the more he had."

Giving while you're living is a good way of knowing where it's going.

UNUSED MONEY

The *Wall Street Journal,* a paper devoted to the discussion of finance, described money as "an article which may be used as a universal passport to everywhere except Heaven, and as a universal provider of everything except happiness."[2]

If money is to be useful . . . it must be used. Henry Ford said, "Money is like an arm or leg . . . you either use it or lose it."

The Dead Sea, in southern Israel, is a forty-seven mile long lake fed by the Jordan River. No animal life exists in its waters. It is the Dead Sea because it only takes in and never gives out.

The New Testament includes a poignant phrase about unused money. "The rust of [your riches] shall be a witness against you" (James 5:3 KJV). Rust speaks of disuse. It is a sure sign of inactivity.

Unused money will never clothe the cold or feed the hungry. Unused money will never heal the sick and lift the fallen. Unused money speaks of a faulty stewardship. Unused money witnesses against us.

Of course, it is right and reasonable to retain sufficient

money for the emergencies of life; however, a wise steward *uses* money wisely.

MISUSED MONEY

Keith Nicholson was an average mine worker when he won $500,000 in a British soccer pool. His wife, who never had much money before, announced they were going to "spend, spend, spend." The Nicholsons bought a house, two cars, and several television sets. They began to give parties weekly. Before long they spent half of their newfound wealth. "We had oodles of money," reported Mrs. Nicholson, "and we set the place alight, but soon we lost our friends. The people we had known in the old days just stopped coming to see us."

Soon the Nicholsons lost all of their wealth, as well as their friends, largely because of misuse.

The way we use our money, over and above our needs, reveals a lot about us. The person who picks up the newspaper and immediately turns to the financial page probably has some money tied up in stocks and bonds. A large annual expenditure for clothing reveals a strong interest in personal appearance. It's true that where your dollars go is where your interests lie. "Where your treasure is, there your heart will be also" (Matthew 6:21).

A friend of mine gives generously to humanitarian causes, especially world missions. Recently, he was asked to report to the local Internal Revenue Service. When questioned about the large sums of money he reported as contributions, my friend produced his canceled checks as proof of his giving. The agent reviewed the checks, and when he was fully convinced that this man actually gave all the money he claimed to have given, he looked at him and said, "You certainly take your faith seriously."

WISELY USED MONEY

The way we give is also the way we will receive. The New Testament book of Luke states it this way, "Give, and it will be given to you: good measure, pressed down, shaken together, and running over . . . for with the same measure that you use, it will be measured back to you" (6:38).

A measure was a unit like a pint, quart, or gallon. Some merchants were dishonest while others were stingy. The writer simply says, "The way you give is the way you will receive."

Early in life, I was taught the joys of giving. Even as a boy of ten selling magazines and later as a teenager working on a milk truck, I tithed 10 percent of my earnings (Malachi 3:10). When my wife and I launched our marriage fifty-five years ago, we agreed to begin giving a tithe of 10 percent and to increase that amount as we prospered (1 Corinthians 16:2). Giving has brought us great joy.

Let me tell you about a man who used his money wisely. More than one hundred years ago, before the Quaker Oats Company existed, a group of millers in Ravenna, Ohio, banded together to change the breakfast menu of America. Until then, the familiar rolled oats we now drench with milk were fed almost exclusively to livestock. Moving those oats from feed silos to our breakfast bowls was a monumental job. The infant industry desperately needed someone with marketing and organizational know-how, and that someone was Henry Crowell.

Henry Crowell came from a well-to-do New England family that, despite its good fortune, was plagued by chronic tuberculosis. At age nine, young Henry stood at his father's grave, lonely and afraid.

After the pastor spoke the words of committal, young Henry

asked to talk with him about life and death. The next day the two knelt in the minister's study as the boy decided to become a Christian.

At seventeen, Crowell himself was stricken with tuberculosis, which had killed four family members already. Doctors told young Crowell to quit school and forget his plans to attend college.

For two years, he rested and worked as a part-time show salesman in the firm his father founded. During those years, D. L. Moody spoke at their Cleveland church. Mr. Moody spoke about how God changed his life through the words of Henry Varley: "The world has yet to see what God can do with, and for, and through, a man who is fully and wholly consecrated to Him."

"Varley didn't say this person had to be educated," Moody testified that night, "or brilliant, or anything else! Just a person!"

Young Crowell thought, *I'll be one of those people!* With his new commitment, Crowell accepted his ruined school plans as confirmation that God didn't need a brilliant servant, just a yielded one.

Still, Crowell's health continued to deteriorate. The next year, in August 1874, he was told to quit his job and do nothing but rest.

Henry Crowell seriously studied his Bible during this time of poor health. He became fascinated by the frequent reference to the number seven. One night he read a passage in the book of Job. "He shall deliver thee in six troubles: yea, in seven there shall no evil touch thee" (Job 5:19 KJV).

He believed that the Lord was speaking to him, telling him he would not die at an early age. His faith grew as his condition became so critical that the doctor reevaluated his case and made a startling recommendation: "You have to live outdoors for the next seven years."

Crowell acted on the doctor's recommendation and went west to the Dakotas to regain his health. Often he experienced loneliness, especially when his fiancé's mother, believing he was dying, persuaded her daughter to break their engagement. But it wasn't God's will for him to die. Instead, Crowell slowly regained his health.

By the fourth year, he began to use his business sense to buy and sell farmland in South Dakota. But during the last year of his exile, a dry spell shriveled his wheat crop from twenty-five bushels per acre to eleven.

Is God moving me from farming? Crowell wondered. Within days, a man offered to buy his prize-winning Percheron horses, as well as his land, allowing Crowell to return to Cleveland. "I felt that I was not in good health," he wrote, "but I would wait and see what God would do next. I knew He would show me what He wanted."

Within thirty days of the sale, a man offered to sell Crowell a Quaker's mill at Ravenna, Ohio. "I doubt if it will make a success," the man admitted. But Crowell thought differently. As early as 1882, Mr. Crowell outlined a plan for his newly acquired mill: "To make better oatmeal than has ever been made, and to combine such companies as are interested and willing into a chartered company."

Crowell's plans were big: "The general company should displace old names with a single trade marker. To this end, it must do educational work, and create an oat demand where none exists. It is only by such a broad distribution and central management that we can avoid the perils of panic, competition, or disaster to some one plant or other."

His plan was so innovative that it took him twenty-five years to convince the small mill owners to give up their petty rivalries and organize under the Quaker Oats Company. Those were twenty-five years of patient waiting and gentle determination.

In 1888, the Crowell family moved from Cleveland to Chicago because the general office of the Oats Millers Association was established there.

Ten years later, the Crowell family came under the teaching of William R. Newell. His teaching revolutionized the lives of the Crowell family. At the same time, the Quaker Oats Company was revolutionizing the world's breakfast habits. By 1910, Quaker became a world organization, the first American food processor to reach this pinnacle.

Once his fortune was made, Crowell became a businessman who believed "a man's business is not chiefly his way of making a living, but his altar where he serves."[3] His stewardship focused on three areas: his time, his money, and his social action. For more than forty years, he gave 65 percent of his income and a great deal of his time to Christian work. He used his money wisely.

The vow young Henry Crowell made lasted more than seventy years 'til his death. At age fifty-five, Mr. Crowell wrote on his desk pad, "If my life can always be lived, so as to please Him, I will be superbly happy."

Crowell did most of his giving while living; however, he also established a trust that aids nonprofit organizations to this day. He wisely used money.

Do your giving while you're living . . .
then you're knowing where it's going.

Lord, grant that my last hour may be my best hour.

OLD ENGLISH PRAYER

*If we really think that home is elsewhere and that
this life is a "wandering to find home,"
why should we not look forward to the arrival?*

C. S. LEWIS[1]

*Death is the great adventure beside which moon landings
and space trips . . . pale into insignificance.*

JOSEPH BAYLY

*So he passed over, and all the trumpets
sounded for him . . . on the other side.*

JOHN BUNYAN, FROM *The Pilgrim's Progress*

In the theological phrase we "make up our souls";
this is the great achievement that makes death the
completion of something that has become a unity,
with a quality of accomplishment and significance
for ourselves and those around us. This is what
makes age not a burden and a defeat, but marvelously
enjoyable in spite of the limitations of the aging body.

WAYNE BOOTH

Happy and wise are those who endeavor to be during
this life . . . as they wish to be found at their death.
Apply yourself so to live now, that at the hour of death,
you may be glad and unafraid.

THOMAS Á. KEMPIS

A man I know found out last year he had terminal cancer.
He was a doctor and knew about dying, and he didn't want
to make his family and friends suffer through that with
him. So he kept his secret. And died. Everybody
said how brave he was to bear his suffering in
silence and not tell anybody. But privately
his family and friends said how angry they were
that he didn't need them, didn't trust their strength.
And it hurt that he didn't say good-bye.

ROBERT FULGHUM[2]

11

FINISHING
WITH GRACE

D ying is something we all have to do. But how well
do we do it?

My predecessor William Culbertson served as the
fifth president of Chicago's famed Moody Bible Institute. Occasionally he would tell the students that he
prayed he would live his life in such a way that he could
"die well."

I was privileged to work with him and to watch him
live out his final days. I had the honor of being his pastor and of serving as a trustee under his leadership. In
1971, I learned he was struggling with lung cancer.
However, outwardly he appeared vigorous, and I felt
that with medical care and divine intervention he
would recover. Early in 1971, the trustee board asked if
I would succeed him as president. In summer 1971, his

physical condition declined rapidly, yet neither his family nor friends felt that his death was imminent.

September was particularly difficult for him. On October 6, he entered the Swedish Covenant Hospital for a series of treatments. The cancer advanced with vengeance, making each day increasingly difficult. On the day of his death, November 16, he shared a favorite verse with several, "Alleluia! For the Lord God Omnipotent reigns" (Revelation 19:6). However, none of us, as I recall, felt this was the last day of his life. After the visitors left, shortly before midnight, he spoke quietly as though he were speaking directly to his Maker, "God, God— yes!" With that, he closed his eyes in death. His prayer was answered; he died well and he finished with grace.

I too desire to die well, and if possible to help my loved ones and friends die well, too.

ENDING WELL

Francis of Assisi, the thirteenth-century Italian evangelist, lived a modest life of poverty even though he was the son of a wealthy textile merchant. His final days were remarkable. Francis asked his doctor how long could he expect to live. When told that his condition was incurable and death would soon arrive, Francis, with great joy, raised his hands to welcome death. After bidding farewell to family and friends, he wrote a few letters. Sensing the end was near, he asked his doctor to announce the arrival of death. Said Francis, "Death will open the door of life," and then he softly quoted Psalm 142:7, "Bring my soul out of prison, that I may praise Your name." He struggled to sing:

Death is our sister, we praise You for Death
Who releases the soul to the light of Your gaze;
And dying we call with the last of our breath
Our thanks . . . and our praise.

Francis died . . . singing!

William Blake, the eighteenth-century artist/poet is heralded as one of England's greatest. His father, a London stocking maker, recognized his son's talent and enrolled him at age ten in art study. From the start Blake displayed strong mystical tendencies, which eventually dominated his life's work.

Blake enjoyed a remarkable marriage to Catherine Boucher. On the day of his death, he called for Catherine to sit beside him and said, "Kate, you have been a good wife; I will draw your portrait." As she sat by his bedside, he sketched and sang with great joy, songs of triumph and hallelujahs. He rejoiced because as he was dying; he sensed that he had "fought a good fight" and finished the race and soon would achieve the goal.

Just before he died, his face glowed, his eyes sparkled, and he began to sing about what he saw in heaven. Blake . . . died well.

A contemporary, Willie Mae Smith, exclaimed as death was approached, "I'm getting ready to go. How am I doing it? I'm laying aside every weight and sin that does so easily beset me . . . and I'm getting light for the flight."

For people of faith, death is an experience to prepare for and befriend. Henry Nouwen asks, "Can we wait for our death as for a friend who wants to welcome us home?"[3]

LIFE'S CERTAINTY

In life we prepare for many contingencies; however, "death" is not a contingency but a certainty. Birth and death circle us, like a challenging moat.

Novelist Somerset Maugham tells of an Arabian merchant who sent his servant to the city of Baghdad to buy provisions. While in the marketplace, the servant saw Death, who appeared to point at him. In panic, the servant fled to tell his master of the encounter. He asked for the use of a horse so he could escape to the distant town of Samara.

Later that day, the merchant also visited the Baghdad marketplace. Seeing "Death" he asked, "Why did you make a threatening gesture at my servant this morning?" Death answered, "That wasn't a threatening gesture, but rather a start of surprise. I was astonished to see him here in Baghdad because tonight I have an appointment with him in the far-off town of Samara."

Alan Seeger (1888–1916), Harvard graduate and poet, enlisted in the French Legion during World War I. He wrote this poem almost two years before he was mortally wounded on July 4, 1919. Alan Seeger anticipated his personal appointment with death.

I HAVE A RENDEZVOUS WITH DEATH

I have a rendezvous with Death,
At some disputed barricade,
When Spring comes back with rustling shade
And apple-blossoms fill the air—
I have a rendezvous with Death

When Spring brings back blue days and fair.
It may be he shall take my hand
And lead me into his dark land
And close my eyes and quench my breath—

It may be I shall pass him still.
I have a rendezvous with Death
On some scarred slope of battered hill,
When Spring comes round again this year
And the first meadow-flowers appear.

God knows 'twere better to be deep
Pillowed in silk and scented down,
Where love throbs out in blissful sleep,
Pulse nigh to pulse, and breath to breath,
Where hushed awakenings are dear—
But I've a rendezvous with Death
At midnight in some flaming town,
When Spring trips north again this year,
And I to my pledged word am true,
I shall not fail that rendezvous.

POEMS BY ALAN SEEGER, 1916[4]

In earlier days people lived with dying in mind, whereas to-day death is the great unmentionable. Psychologists claim the majority of people refuse to face death, even to the point of neglecting a yearly physical checkup, lest they confront their own mortality.

People face death differently. One dies in confidence, while another dies in doubt. Some die rejoicing, while others experience remorse. It was said that when King Jehoram died, "He departed *with no one's regret*" (2 Chronicles 21:20 NASB, italics added). He died wrong because he lived wrong. However, the Scripture says of Abijah that at his death "all Israel mourned for him" (1 Kings 14:18). In spite of heredity and environment, Abijah died right.

TWO WORDS FOR DEATH

For people of biblical faith there are two descriptive words regarding death in the Bible. In 2 Peter 1:15, the word translated "decease" is the Greek word *exodus,* the title of the second book of the Bible. It means "the road out." Death for those of faith is a triumphant exodus . . . like the children of Israel released from the enslavement of Egypt. Death for the believer is a "going out" into God's presence.

In Philippians 1:23, the apostle Paul wrote: "Having a desire to depart and be with Christ, which is far better." The Greek word *depart,* means "to loose." The picture is of an anchor being lifted, freeing the boat to sail beyond the horizon into the unseen harbor. Death for those of faith is an anchors aweigh.

Malcolm Muggeridge speaks of death with joyful anticipation:

> So, like a prisoner awaiting his release, like a school-boy when the end of the term is near, like a migrant bird ready to fly south, like a patient in the hospital anxiously scanning the doctor's face to see whether a discharge may be expected, I long to be gone. Extricating myself from the flesh I have too long inhabited, hearing the key turn in the lock of time so that the great

doors of eternity swing open, disengaging my tired mind from
its interminable conundrums, and my tired ego from its weari-
some insistencies. Such is the prospect of death.

Several years ago, a close family friend named Beverly was
dying from cancer. From the beginning she reflected a radiant
spirit not for healing, but for dying. She had befriended death.
On one occasion she showed my wife and me her proposed fu-
neral service under the caption, "My Praise Service." She had
carefully selected the Scriptures to be read and the songs to be
sung. She requested a period of time, reserved for any in the
audience to share in a voluntary, impromptu way, whatever
they wanted to share.

On one occasion I tried to comfort her husband Alan, assuring him of our prayers and friendship. To which he replied,
"George, if Bev were going to Hawaii, wouldn't you be happy
for her?"

"Yes, of course," I answered.

"Well, heaven is a whole lot better than Hawaii." Beverly's
faith was anchored to the Resurrection (2 Corinthians 4:14).
The confidence of a future resurrection gave Beverly a hope-
filled perspective. This is an anchor for aging.

D. L. Moody, while speaking to a large New York City
gathering said, "Someday you will read in the papers that
Moody is dead. Don't you believe a word of it. At that moment
I shall be more alive than I am now. . . . I was born of the flesh
in 1837, I was born of the spirit in 1855. That which is born of
the flesh will die. That which is born of the spirit shall live for-
ever." How could a person be so confident? Only because of
faith in a future resurrection.

Each passing year our children find it challenging to buy

my wife and me a Christmas gift. Our needs are simple. Several years ago they purchased for me *The Oxford Book of Aging*. I think they were trying to tell me something. I enjoyed the book, especially the poetry. I was lifted and challenged by the poem by Sterling Brown, an African-American. His wife had just died, and he writes to her in the old Negro dialect, instructing her about a future eternal home.

> *Honey*
> *When de man*
> *Calls out de las' train*
> *You're gonna ride*
> *Tell him howdy.*
>
> *Gather up yo' basket*
> *An' yo' knittin' an' yo' things.*
> *An' go on up an' visit*
> *Wid frien' Jesus fo' a spell.*
>
> *Show Marfa*
> *How to make yo' green grape jellies,*
> *An' give po' Lazarus*
> *A passel of them Golden Biscuits.*
>
> *Scald some meal*
> *Fo' some righdown good spoonbread*
> *Fo' Li'l box-plunkin' David.*
>
> *An' sit aroun'*
> *An' tell them Hebrew Chillen*
> *All yo' stories . . .*

Honey
Don't be feared of them pearly gates.
Don't go 'round to de back,
No mo' dataway
Not evah no mo'.

Let Michael tote yo' burden
An' yo' pocketbook an' evahthing
'Cept yo' Bible,
While Gabriel blows somp'n
Solemn but loudsome
On dat horn of his'n.

Honey
Go straight on to de Big House,
An' speak to yo' God
Widout no fear an' tremblin'.

Then sit down
An' pass de time of day awhile.

Give a good talkin' to
To yo' favorite 'postle Peter,
An' rub the po' head
Of mixed-up Judas,
An' joke awhile wid Jonah.

Then, when you gits de chance,
Always rememberin' yo' raisin',
Let 'em know youse tired

Jest a mite tired.
Jesus will find yo' bed fo' you
Won't no servant evah bother wid yo' room.
Jesus will lead you
To a room wid windows
Openin' on cherry trees an' plum trees
Bloomin' everlastin'.

An' dat will be yours,
Fo' keeps,
Den take yo' time . . .
Honey, take yo' bressed time.

STERLING A BROWN[5]

J. I. Packer reminds us, "Dying well is one of the good works to which Christians are called, and He will enable us who serve Him, *to die well.*" We can finish with grace.

12

QUOTATIONS ON
AGING AND DYING

THE LIGHTER SIDE OF AGING

It's nice to be here; when you're 99 years old it's nice to be anywhere.

GEORGE BURNS

A joyous occasion is never quite as wonderful as when it becomes a memory.

PRESIDENT JIMMY CARTER
Virtues of Aging, 22

Life begins at 40—but so do fallen arches, rheumatism, faulty eyesight, and the tendency to tell a story to the same person, three or four times.

BILL FEATHER

Children are a great help. They are a comfort in your old age. And they help you reach it faster, too.

ANONYMOUS

There are three ages to mankind: youth, middle age, and . . . my, you're looking good.

MARIE STOPES

He's so old . . . his blood type was discontinued.

BILL DANA

You can take no credit for beauty at 16. But if you are beautiful at 60, it will be your soul's own doing.

MARIE STOPES

Whatever poet, orator, or sage may say of it, old age is still old age.

SINCLAIR LEWIS

To me—old age is fifteen years older than I am.

BERNARD MANNES BARUCH

Old age is when you know all the answers . . . but nobody asks you any questions.

LAWRENCE J. PETER

I'm 65 and I guess that puts me in with the geriatrics, but if there were fifteen months in every year, I'd only be 52.

JAMES THURBER

Old friends are best. King James used to call for his old shoes; they were the easiest for his feet.

WAYNE BOOTH

[When David Ben-Gurion came out of retirement for the ninth time, he was asked by an American why he bothered to retire.]
"It's like those 'going out of business' signs you see along Seventh Avenue—a chance to unload stock he doesn't want, hire a new staff, and make a different contract with the union."

DAVID BEN-GURION

Life is 10 percent what you make it and 90 percent how you take it.

IRVING BERLIN

My grandfather would look through the obituary columns and say to me, "Strange, isn't it, how everybody seems to die in alphabetical order."

JACKIE VERNON

If you are over the hill, why not enjoy the view?

MACK MCGINNIS

By the time a man gets to greener pastures he can't climb the fence.

FRANK DICKSON

I'm not getting old. My mirror is just getting wrinkled.

ANONYMOUS

Old age: When actions creak louder than words.

DANA ROBBINS

When a man's friends begin to compliment him about looking younger, he may be sure that they think he is growing old.

WASHINGTON IRVING

I will not make age an issue . . . I am not going to exploit for political purposes my opponent's youth and inexperience.

RONALD REAGAN

At age 73 concerning his 56-year-old opponent, Walter Mondale

October 21, 1984, debate

✺ SERIOUS QUOTATIONS ABOUT AGING

We believe that aging is not a reason for despair but a basis for hope, not a slow decaying but a gradual maturing, not a fate to be undergone but a chance to be embraced.

HENRY J. M. NOUWEN & WALTER GAFFNEY

Aging: The Fulfilment of Life

New York: Image Book, Doubleday, 1976, 20

Preparation for old age should begin not later than one's teens. A life which is empty of purpose until 65 will not suddenly become filled on retirement.

ARTHUR MORGAN

People are anxious to save up financial means for old age; they should also be anxious to prepare a spiritual means for old age. . . . Wisdom, maturity, tranquility do not come all of a sudden when we retire.

ABRAHAM JOSHUA HERSCHEL

If a thing is old, it is a sign that it was fit to live. Old families, old customs, old styles survive because they are fit to survive. The guarantee of continuity is quality. Submerge the good in a flood of the new, and the good will come back to join the good which the new brings with it. Old-fashioned hospitality, old-fashioned politics, old-fashioned honor in business had qualities of survival. These will come back.

ANONYMOUS

What if someone had decided that Pablo Picasso, Pablo Casals, or Michelangelo, still producing in their 80s and 90s, had "no future" when they became 70 years old?

MARGARET C. ELWELL

Age should not have its face lifted, but it should rather teach the world to admire wrinkles as the etchings of experience and the firm line of character.

RALPH BARTON PERRY

The cure for age is interest and enthusiasm and work. . . . Life's evening will take its character from the day which has preceded it. You will always find joy in the evening . . . if you've spent the day well.

GEORGE MATHESON

Old age is just as important and meaningful a part of God's perfect will as is youth. God is every bit as interested in the old as the young.

J. O. SANDERS

Dr. E. Stanley Jones suggested the following steps for continuing growth in old age:

1. *Don't retire. Change your occupation . . . do something you have always wanted to do.*
2. *Learn something new every day.*
3. *Set yourself to be gracious to someone every day.*
4. *Don't let yourself grow negative; be positive.*
5. *Look around you for something for which to be grateful every day. Gratitude will become a settled habit.*
6. *Now that your bodily activities are slowing down, let your spiritual activities increase. Old age provides increased opportunity for prayer.*
7. *Keep laying up as the years come and go to "the good store" of which Jesus spoke. This "good store" is the depository of every thought, motive, action, attitude which we drop into the subconscious mind. It can be the deep subsoil into which we can strike our roots in old age and blossom at the end like a night-blooming cereus.*

E. STANLEY JONES,

Growing Spiritually

Nashville: Abington, 1953, 313

Your manner of life now is already determining your life in those years of old age and retirement, without your realizing it even, and perhaps without your giving enough thought to it. One must therefore prepare oneself for retirement.

PAUL TOURNIER,

Learn to Grow

Louisville: Westminster/John Knox Press, 1972, 13

In order to make a success of old age, one must begin it earlier, and not try to postpone it as long as possible. In the middle of life we must stop to think, to organize our existence with an eye to a still distant future, instead of allowing ourselves to be entirely sucked into the professional and social whirl. It is then that it is important to give place little by little to less external activities, less technical and more cultural, which will survive the moment of retirement.

PAUL TOURNIER,

Learn to Grow

Louisville: Westminster/John Knox Press, 1972, 12

It is only logical that if God's will is good and acceptable and perfect (Romans 12:2), then complaining about it or rebelling against it is out. If God's will is acceptable, it must be accepted.

J. O. SANDERS

ON WAKING IN PRISON

O God, early in the morning I cry to You
Help me to pray
And to concentrate my thoughts on You:
I cannot do this alone.
In me there is darkness,
But with You there is light;
I am lonely, but You do not leave me;
I am feeble in heart, but with You there is help;
I am restless, but with You there is peace.
In me there is bitterness, but with You there is patience;
I do not understand Your ways,
But You know the way for me.

DIETRICH BONHOEFFER (1906–1945),

while awaiting execution in a Nazi prison

⁀ DEATH

You haven't lost anything when you know where it is. Death can hide but not divide.

VANCE HAVNER

I'm not afraid to die. I'm looking forward to it. I know the Lord has His arms wrapped around this big sparrow.

ETHEL WATERS

Life is a hard fight, a struggle, a wrestling with the principle of evil, hand to hand, foot to foot. Every inch of the way is disputed. The night is given us to take breath, to pray, to drink deep at the fountain of power. The day, to use the strength which has been given us, to go forth to work with it till the evening.

FLORENCE NIGHTINGALE

Since General MacArthur made his famous statement, "Old soldiers never die, they just fade away," interesting quotations have been proposed. Such as,
> *Old postmen never die, they just lose their Zip.*
> *Old scoutmasters never die, they just smell that way.*
> *Old deans never die, they just lose their faculties.*
> *Old doctors never die, they just lose their patience.*

ANONYMOUS

Every man must do two things alone; he must do his own believing and his own dying.

MARTIN LUTHER

The measure of a life, after all, is not its duration but its donation.

CORRIE TEN BOOM

If you draw near the end in somber circumstances, remember that as a faithful child of God you await promotion. Who knows but that the brightest jewel in your crown is for that lonely afternoon and night when all seemed lost but you believed anyway. Remember John the Baptist in prison and John on Patmos and countless millions who have been on that road before you. Remember Mr. Fearing in Bunyan's immortal Pilgrim's Progress, *who dreaded Jordan all his days. But when he reached it, the water was a record low, and he got across "not much above wet-shod." The last chapter in life can be the best.*

VANCE HAVNER

As a well-spent day brings happy sleep, so life well used brings happy death.

LEONARDO DA VINCI

Lord Jesus Christ,
You are the only source of health for the living, and You promise eternal life to the dying. I entrust myself to Your holy will. If You wish me to stay longer in this world, I pray that You will heal me of my present sickness. If You wish me to leave this world, I readily lay aside this mortal body, in the sure hope of receiving an immortal body which shall enjoy everlasting health. I ask only that You relieve me of pain, that whether I live or die, I may rest peaceful and contented.

ERASMUS (1469–1536)
Book of Prayers

What is dying? Just what it is to put off a garment. For the body is about the soul as a garment; and after laying this aside for a short time by means of death, we shall resume it again with more splendor.

ST. JOHN CHRYSOSTOM (347–407),

Early Christian saint

Death always waits. The door of the hearse is never closed.

JOSEPH BAYLY

God buries His workmen but carries on His work.

CHARLES WESLEY

Because I could not stop for death
He kindly stopped for me;
The carriage held but just ourselves
And immortality.

EMILY ELIZABETH DICKINSON

Edythe Draper, *Draper's Book of Quotations,*

Wheaton, IL: Tyndale House, 1990, 127.

Christ taught an astonishing thing about physical death: not merely that it is an experience robbed of its terror but that as an experience it does not exist at all. To "sleep in Christ," like one that wraps the drapery of his couch about him, and lies down to pleasant dreams.

WILLIAM CULLEN BRYANT

When Michelangelo, already well along in years, was discussing life with an old friend, the latter commented, "Yes, after such a good life, it's hard to look death in the eye." "Not at all!" contradicted Michelangelo. "Since life was such a pleasure, death coming from the same great Source cannot displease us."

TEMMLER WERKE

I don't know what your destiny will be, but one thing I know, the only ones among you who will be really happy are those who have sought and found how to serve.

ALBERT SCHWEITZER

Don't allow yourself to feel old; don't give up your interest in life; cultivate a hobby; have a game now and then with your grandchildren, or someone else's; don't think about the end—God has lovingly planned that, and you will be as unaware of your passing out as you were of your coming.

F. B. MEYER

THE OLD PLAYER
Call him not old, whose visionary brain
Holds o'er the past its undivided reign.
For him in vain the envious seasons roll
Who bears eternal summer in his soul.

OLIVER WENDELL HOLMES

People are reluctant to talk about old age and death because they are afraid of emotion, and they willingly avoid the things they feel most emotional about, though these are the very things they most need to talk about.

PAUL TOURNIER
Learn to Grow Old
Louisville: Westminster/John Knox Press, 1972, 217

Christian faith does not involve repressing one's anxiety in order to appear strong. On the contrary, it means recognizing one's weakness, accepting the inward truth about oneself, confessing one's anxiety, and still to believe, that is to say that the Christian puts his trust not in his own strength, but in the grace of God.

PAUL TOURNIER
Learn to Grow Old
Louisville: Westminster/John Knox Press, 1972, 222

I will say with Lorenzo de Medici that those who do not hope for another life are always dead to this one.

GOETHE

Of dying C. S. Lewis said, "You needn't worry about not feeling brave. Our Lord didn't. . . . Remember the scene in Gethsemane. How thankful I am that when God became man, He did not choose to become a man of iron nerves; that would not have helped weaklings like you and me nearly so much."

THE QUOTABLE LEWIS
Letters of C. S. Lewis, 1953

❦

NOTES

Chapter 1: Lighten Up

1. George Sweeting, *Who Said That?* (Chicago: Moody, 1994), 30.
2. Dr. David Weeks and Jamie James, *Secrets of the Super Young* (New York: Villard Books/Random House, 1998), 23–24.
3. Ibid.
4. *Esquire*, March 2001, 143.

Chapter 2: People of Faith Tend to Live Longer

1. Donald H. Kausler and Barry C. Kausler, *The Graying of America* 2nd ed. (Univ. of Illinois, 2001), 339–40.
2. Marilyn Elias, "Widow of Sept. 11 hero carries on; She says God has a plan, and it put Todd Beamer on Flight 93," *USA Today*, 21 November 2001, D13.
3. David Snowdon, Ph.D., *Aging with Grace* (New York: Random House Bantam , 2001), 202.
4. Thomas T. Perls and Margery Hutter Silver, *Living to 100: Lessons in Living to Your Maximum Potential at Any Age* (New York: Persens Books, 1999), 77.

5. Kausler, *The Graying of America*, 236–37.

6. Snowdon, *Aging with Grace*, 202.

7. Kausler, *The Graying of America*, 340.

8. Dr. Herbert Benson, *Beyond the Relaxation Response,* (New York: Berkley, 1985).

9. D. O. Moberg, *Aging and Spirituality* (Birmingham, NY: Haworth Pastoral Press, 2001), 67.

10. Robert Burns, *The Poetical Works of Burns* (Boston: Houghton-Mifflen, 1974), 223.

Chapter 3: Temple Keeping

1. John W. Rowe and Robert L. Kahn, *Successful Aging* (New York: Pantheon, 1999), 50.

2. Bill Cosby, *Time Flies* (New York: Bantam, 1988), 35–39.

3. *Staying Well* (New York: Random House, 1986), 70.

4. Kausler, *The Graying of America*, 177.

5. Ibid., 59.

6. Dale Carnegie, *How to Stop Worrying and Start Living* (New York: Pocket Books, 1984), 4.

Chapter 4: The Age Boom

1. Peter G. Peterson, *Gray Dawn* (New York: Time Books, 1999), 3.

2. Ibid., 1.

3. Jimmy Carter, *Virtues of Aging* (New York: Time Books, 1998), 28.

Chapter 5: Aging with Joy

1. Morton Puner, *To the Good Long Life* (New York: Universe Books, 1974).

2. Anne Morrow Lindbergh, *Gift from the Sea* (New York: Random House, 1955), 35.

Chapter 6: Arteries Plus Attitude

1. Michael F. Roizen, M.D., *Real Age: Are You As Young As You Can Be?*, (New York, Cliff Street Books, 1999), 59.

Chapter 7: Why Comedians Live So Long

1. Thomas T. Perls and Margery Hutter Silver, *Living to 100*, 72.

2. *Executive Digest: Lessons in Living to Your Maximum Potential at Any Age* (New York: Persens Books, 1999).

3. Leslie B. Flynn, *Serve Him with Mirth*, (Grand Rapids: Zondervan, 1960), 14–15.

4. Ibid., 44.

5. Ibid., 19.

Chapter 9: Nothing to Fear . . . but Fear Itself

1. Rick Hampton, "Fear as a weapon: Terrorist tactics rarely triumph; But hijackings, anthrax scares and other threats have rattled many in the home of the brave," *USA Today*, 1 November, 2001, Sec. 1A and 2A.

2. Alfons Deeken, *Growing Old* (New York: Paulist, 1972), 99.

3. Wayne Booth, *The Art of Growing Older* (New York: Poseidon Press, 1992), 275.

Chapter 10 : Do Your Giving While You're Living

1. Dallas Willard, *The Spirit of the Disciplines* (New York: HarperCollins, 1988), 217.

2. *Wall Street Journal*.

3. Richard E. Day, *A Christian in Big Business: The Life Story of Henry Parsons Crowell* (Chicago: Moody, 1954).

Chapter 11: Finishing with Grace

1. Edythe Draper, *Draper's Book of Quotations* (Wheaton, IL: Tyndale, 1992).

2. Ibid., 131.

3. Henry Nouwen, *Our Greatest Gift* (New York: HarperCollins, 1995), xiii.

4. Franklyn B. Snyder and Edward D. Snyder, *A Book of American Literature* (New York: MacMillan, 1935), 1096.

5. Sterling A. Brown, *The Oxford Book of Aging* (New York: Oxford Univ., 1994).

A Generous Impulse

ISBN: 0-8024-4024-X

With love as the hallmark of his decades of ministry, Dr. Sweeting has a story that stands as a beacon to young people willing to totally commit themselves to Christ. This is the story of his upbringing in a godly Scottish-American home, his conversion to Christ and call to the ministry as a young person, his emergence as an evangelist, pastor and finally head of one of the leading Christian institutions in the world.

One of his themes over the years has been *"Never suppress a generous impulse"* and has benefited friends, coworkers, subordinates, parishioners, and even detractors.

Jerry Jenkins is the author of more than 100 books, including the best-selling *Left Behind* Series. His writing has also appeared in *Reader's Digest, Parade,* American and United in-flight magazines, and dozens of Christian periodicals. Jerry also assisted Dr. Billy Graham with his memoirs, *Just As I Am*, a New York Times bestseller.

MOODY
The Name You Can Trust
1-800-678-8812 **www.MoodyPress.org**

How to Begin the Christian Life

Beginnings—they're crucial! Houses need strong foundations. Races are won by strong starts just as much as by fast finishes.

The beginning of the Christian life is no different. A strong start to your Christian life is not only pleasing to our Lord but will help equip you for what lies ahead. The future will be exciting—but challenging. Will you be ready? *How To Begin the Christian Life* is a modern classic. With more than 400,000 copies in print it already helped tens of thousands begin their Christian lives. Now let it help you or someone that you know. This little handbook will give you reliable scriptural guidance in these and other areas of Christian living.

ISBN: 0-8024-3581-5

How to Continue the Christian Life

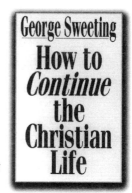

"Any book that Dr. Sweeting writes has my highest recommendation. This book will be a blessing and an encouragement in your own life, but also a tool you can give to help others grow in Christ."
—Dr. Billy Graham

"Christianity is not just a beginning ... at its best it's an all consuming focus of life. At last a book that gets us beyond first things to the biblical formulas for growth and discovery. And, who better to write it than my friend, George Sweeting."
—Dr. Joseph Stowell, President of Moody Bible Institute.

ISBN: 0-8024-3587-4

MOODY
The Name You Can Trust
1-800-678-8812 www.MoodyPress.org

If you are interested in information
about other books written from a
biblical perspective, please write
to the following address:

Northfield Publishing
215 West Locust Street
Chicago, IL 60610